RUM & REGGAE'S
CUBA
Havana and beyond

Rum&Reggae's
Cuba
Havana and Beyond

by

Jonathan Runge

RUM & REGGAE GUIDEBOOKS, Inc. •
Prides Crossing, Massachusetts • 2002

ISBN: 1-893675-03-3
LIBRARY OF CONGRESS CATALOG CARD NUMBER: 2001119638

Book design by Scott-Martin Kosofsky and Betsy Sarles at The Philidor Company, Cambridge, MA

Cover design by Betsy Sarles & Jonathan Runge

Maps by Tony Lulek and Bruce Withey
Printed in Canada on recycled paper

For Duncan and Tom

CONTENTS

CUBA

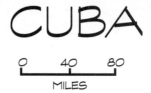

0   40   80
MILES

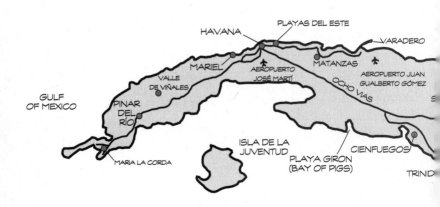

PLAYAS DEL ESTE

HAVANA

VARADERO

MARIEL

MATANZAS

AEROPUERTO
JOSÉ MARTÍ

AEROPUERTO JUAN
GUALBERTO GÓMEZ

VALLE
DE VIÑALES

OCHO VÍAS

GULF
OF MEXICO

PINAR
DEL
RÍO

ISLA DE LA
JUVENTUD

CIENFUEGOS

MARIA LA CORDA

PLAYA GIRON
(BAY OF PIGS)

TRINID

FLORIDA

CAYO COCO

ATLANTIC
OCEAN

CIEGO
DE ÁVILA

CAMAGÜEY

LAS TUNAS

HOLGUÍN

BARACOA

BAYAMO

GUANTÁNAMO

SANTIAGO
DE CUBA

GUANTÁNAMO
BAY NAS

CARIBBEAN SEA

N

PREFACE

RUM & REGGAE'S *Cuba* is the sixth book to be published by Rum & Reggae Guidebooks, Inc. Writing these books is now a team effort. For *Rum & Reggae's Cuba,* Jean Kim Chaix and Diane Lulek were contributors.

- ☞ Jean Kim Chaix is a freelance writer and television producer who was born in France and raised in Managua, Nicaragua.
- ☞ Diane Lulek is an artist, photographer, freelance travel writer and mother of four. She has traveled to Europe, the Caribbean, South America, Africa, and extensively in North America.

We hope you enjoy the book. Please be sure to visit our Web site at www.rumreggae.com.

ACKNOWLEDGMENTS

Writing a book on Cuba is a real challenge, from travel to and from it to obtaining accurate and reliable information. It's kind of like talking on a cell phone where every other word is dropped or garbled (we can relate to the Sprint commercials). We did not spend our days on the beach or by the pool sipping a rum punch. Well, okay, sometimes we did. But most of the time we were running around checking out this or that and complaining about the heat, all within the confines of organized cultural tours. We weren't as footloose and fancy-free as we are normally accustomed to being when we do research.

Fortunately, some wonderful people helped us out along the way. We'd like to take this opportunity to sincerely thank those who did. In no particular order, they are Amy Giacalone, Geoff Davis, and Duncan Donahue and Tom Fortier. If we overlooked your name, sorry, but thanks for your help!

Rum & Reggae's Cuba is published by Rum & Reggae Guidebooks, Inc. I have a lot of helpers, and all deserve a hearty thanks. First and foremost, a lot of credit for this book goes to Jean Kim Chaix, who did the original work for Rum & Reggae, and Diane Lulek, our update maven. My warmest gratitude also goes to the following: our wonderful book designers, Betsy Sarles and Scott-Martin Kosofsky; our very talented Web designer, Michael Carlson; our corporate illustrator and animation megastar, Eric Orner; our cartographers Bruce Withey and Tony Lulek; our distributor, Midpoint Trade Books and its great staff, Gail Kump, Eric Kampf, Chris Bell, and Julie Borgelt; our printer, Transcontinental Printing, and its terrific rep, Ed Catania; and our patient copy editor and indexer, Judith Antonelli.

There were several people who helped in other ways. Many thanks to Nan Garland, Elvis Jiménez-Chávez and Chris Lawrence, Tom Jonsson, and Gedy Moody.

Finally, wicked thanks to our not-so-new-but-not-yet-tired staff members, Joe Shapiro—the Director of Marketing and Sales and a Brazil nut; and Lauren White, copy editor, proofreader, and all-around great gal. Tons of thanks also to my business partner and right-hand man, Tony Lulek; and to my parents, Eunice and Albert Runge, for their continued enthusiasm and support.

And a can of dolphin-safe tuna to my cat and guardian angel, Jada.

To all who helped, many thanks—YAH MON!

Jonathan Runge
Author and Publisher
Rum & Reggae Guidebooks, Inc.
Prides Crossing, Massachusetts
March 1, 2002

INTRODUCTION

OUR MIDDLE NAME IS BITCH.™ That's how we describe our distinct point of view. *Rum & Reggae's Cuba* is not your typical tourist guidebook to the birthplace of the *mojito*. We like to say that the Rum & Reggae series is written for people who want more out of a vacation than the standard tourist fare. Our reader is more sophisticated and independent. He's also more active—be it scuba diving, windsurfing, speaking Spanish, hiking, sailing, golfing, playing tennis, exploring, or cocktailing. Or she's more particular, in search of places that are secluded, cerebral, spiritual, or très branché (if you have to ask what the latter means, those places are not for you).

This book differs from other guidebooks in another way. Instead of telling you that everything is "nice"—nice, that is, for the average Joe—*Rum & Reggae's Cuba* offers definitive opinions. We will tell you what's fantastic and what's not, from the point of view of someone who loathes the tourist label and the other bland travel books whose names we won't mention.

We take you to the jewel of the Caribbean, Havana, and beyond. We will tell you *how* you can do it and share our recommendations of where to go (and where not to go). More importantly, we filter out all the crap for you so you can have fun reading the book and enjoy your vacation and keep the decision making and hassles to a minimum. We wish we had this book when we were doing our research. It would have made our job a helluva lot easier. We would have had more time to kick back and get sand between our toes.

So mix yourself a stiff *mojito*, put on some Buena Vista Social club, and sit back and let *Rum & Reggae's Cuba* take you on your own private voyage to Cuban heat.

BEFORE YOU GO

Warning for U.S. Citizens

Technically it is not illegal for U.S. citizens to travel to Cuba, but under the Trading With the Enemy Act, U.S. citizens and people under the jurisdiction of the United States are legally forbidden to spend money—dollars or any other currency—in Cuba. This includes any payment for accommodations, food, airline tickets, taxis, goods and services, etc. Criminal penalties for violating the sanctions can range upward from 10 years in prison and up to $250,000 in fines. Exceptions do exist.

The U.S. Department of the Treasury may issue licenses to journalists, researchers, government officials, humanitarian aid workers, and Cuban Americans with relatives in Cuba, for academic excursions and religious missions. U.S. citizens who are fully hosted or sponsored by people not subject to U.S. jurisdiction are permitted to travel to Cuba but must still travel through a third country (i.e., Canada, Mexico, Jamaica, or the Bahamas). The Treasury Department puts the burden of proof of sponsorship on the individual traveler. The traveler will be considered in violation of the sanctions until he or she can provide proper documentation of full sponsorship, including visa and proof of payment of the entry and exit tax. For more details, contact the Office of Foreign Assets Control (OFAC), U.S. Department of the Treasury, 1500 Pennsylvania Avenue NW, Annex Building 2nd floor, Washington, DC 20220, Telephone 202-622-2480, Info-by-Fax at 202-622-0077, or on the Internet at www.treas.gov/ofac.

There is a legitimate way for U.S. citizens who do not have family in Cuba to visit the country. Cultural exchange-study programs are authorized by the U.S. Department of the Treasury, and there are several companies who are licensed by the Treasury's Office of

Foreign Assets Control. These "educational" programs focus on Cuba's history and culture, and trips will have themes like architecture, music, African heritage, dance, the people of Cuba, language study, even Hemingway's Cuba. We recommend them for those Americans who want to see Cuba without Uncle Sam breathing down their neck, and hey, ya might learn something, too! Here are some of the licensed cultural exchange–study organizations who conduct Americans to Cuba tours:

> **Worldguest Travel Services** (www.worldguest.com), 800-873-9691 or 201-861-5059
>
> **Marazul Tours, Inc.** (www.marazultours.com), 800-223-5334 or 201-840-6711
>
> **Cross-Cultural Solutions** (www.traveltocubanow.org), 800-380-4777 or 914-632-0022

For the record, about 164,000 Americans made trips to Cuba in 2001, most of them authorized as nontourists who obtained visas from the Treasury Department. About 27,000 Americans were unauthorized, entering through Canada, Mexico, the Bahamas or Jamaica, rather than via the scheduled charter flights operating out of Miami, New York, and Los Angeles. Hundreds of them came home to a registered letter from the Office of Foreign Assets Control—the same folks responsible for tracking terrorist funds—which accused travelers of violating the Trading With the Enemy Act. Fines average $7,500 (they can go as high as $55,000), but they are also negotiable and one can request an administrative hearing to contest them. Alas, the department that handles these hearings is so backlogged that a new administration may well be in place by the time all these cases are heard (hint, hint). On February 11, 2002, the Senate Appropriations Committee took testimony from individuals who have been fined—Committee Chairman Byron Dorgan (D-ND), called the travel ban "absurd." If you agree (or if you don't), now is the time to make your voice heard with your senator. Remember, it is *not* illegal for Americans to visit the country—freedom to travel is protected under the Constitution—but it *is* against Treasury Department regulations to spend money while on Cuban soil, effectively preventing Americans from legally exploring the country.

Health Issues

The Center for Disease Control will prepare a Travax report for you through your doctor's office, with information regarding required AIDS testing (for those who stay longer than 90 days), recommended immunizations, and general information.

Don't drink the water or anything with ice cubes. Salad is suspect, as it is generally washed in tap water. Even the Cubans boil their drinking water. Bottled water is available everywhere, in small markets, ice cream stands, bars and restaurants, and in the minibars in the hotel rooms. We even brushed our teeth with it.

There are no mosquitos in Havana, but inland areas, away from ocean breezes, have enough to warrant packing bug spray.

Climate

The weather in Cuba varies, depending on what part of the country you are in. The northwestern section, including Havana, often has weather similar to the very southern tip of Florida (it lies barely south of the Tropic of Cancer). Cold fronts from the States do make it here, resulting in some cooler days and nights during the winter. The southeastern part of the island is more tropical. Here, the temperature rarely dips below 70 degrees or scales to above 90 degrees F (at sea level). It gets cooler at night in the country's three mountains ranges (the Sierra Maestra to the southeast, the Sierra del Escambray in the central region, and the Cordillera de los Organos in the west), making it ideal for sleeping. The sun shines almost every day. Rainfall comes in the form of brief, intense cloudbursts, quickly followed by sunshine. It's pretty hard not to get a tan. The only weather peril to a Cuban vacation is an occasional summer tropical depression or hurricane, which can make life very exciting. Many a marriage was ignited when visitors were stranded in a tempest.

There are two basic climate categories in Cuba: lush (very green, hot, somewhat humid, with lots of rainfall) and arid (brown with cactus and very dry). The windward side (the north and east coasts) is the lush, wetter, and greener side. The mountains that traverse the island from southeast to northwest block most of the typical rainfall that comes with the prevailing trade winds. This makes much of the southern coast in the lee of the mountains semi-arid to arid. Vegetation tends scrubby with cactus, although there certainly are enough palm trees around to keep palm tree lovers happy. The western end of Cuba is fairly lush as the mountains on this end of the island are too low to stop the rain.

Both lush and arid climes are warm to hot, depending on the season and the extent of the trade winds. Summer, while only about 5 to 10 degrees hotter than winter, feels much hotter due to the dramatically increased humidity and decreased wind. The one constant is the sun. It is always strong, and will swiftly fry unprotected pale faces—and bodies—to a glowing shade of lobster red.

Building a Base for Tanning

Since the advent of "fake 'n bake" (tanning machines) and pretanning accelerators, there is absolutely no reason to get burned on your first day out in the tropical sun. With some advance attention, you can stay outside for hours on your first day, and let's face it, what you want to do when you step off the plane is hit the beach.

Just about every town has a tanning center with a cutesy name like Tanfastic or Tanfasia. Most health clubs have one or two tanning "coffins" lying around, beckoning pasty skins to look healthier and more attractive in a matter of minutes. Ultraviolet tanning is safer when used properly, because the UVB light doesn't have the severe burning rays of earlier sun lamps or, of course, the sun.

Many of these tanning centers have tanning-prep packages of 10 sessions: you start with about five minutes of "sunning" and work up to 20 or 30. Spread out over the two weeks prior to your departure, this should give you an excellent head start on a great Caribbean tan.

Pretan accelerators, available from a wide variety of manufacturers, chemically stimulate the manufacture of melanin, the pigment that darkens your skin. (Normally it takes direct exposure to the sun to start its production.) A pretan accelerator doesn't change your color or dye your skin like the QT of yesteryear (whoops, we're dating ourselves!). It prepares the skin with extra melanin so that you tan the first time out rather than burn, and much faster too.

What to Wear and Take Along

Less is more. That's the motto to remember when packing to go to the Caribbean. Bring only what you can carry for 10 minutes at a good clip, because you'll often be schlepping your luggage for at least that time, and it's hot. If you haven't already done so, invest in a piece of luggage with wheels.

What you really need to take along are a bathing suit, shorts, T-shirts or tanks, cotton sweater, a pair of sandals, sunglasses, and a Discman. After all, you are on vacation. However, this is the dawn of a new century and people tend to dress up for no reason, so you may want to bring some extra togs to look presentable at the dinner table. To help you be totally prepared (and to make your packing a lot easier), we've assembled a list of essentials for a week.

The Packing List

Clothes
   bathing suit (or two)
   T shirts (4)—You'll end up buying at least one.
   tank tops—They're cooler and show off your muscles or curves.
   polo shirts (2)
   shorts (2)
   nice, compatible lightweight pants (also good for the plane)
   sandals—Those that can get wet, like Tevas, are best.
   cotton sweater or sweatshirt
   undergarments
   sneakers (or good walking shoes) or topsiders (for boaters)
   Women: lightweight dress (most women prefer to bring a
      couple of dresses for evening)
   Men: If you must have a lightweight sport coat, wear it
      (with appropriate shoes) on the plane

Essentials
   toiletries
   sunscreens (SPF 15+, 8, 4 [oil], and lip protector)
   moisturizers (Noxema is still the old standard for sunburn;
      or aloe gel)
   some good books—Don't expect to find a worthwhile read
      at your destination.

Cutter's or Woodsman's insect repellent, or Skin So Soft
   (oh, those nasty bugs)
sunglasses!
hat or visor!
Discman (CDs) or iPod
camcorder or pocket camera (disposables are great for the
   beach and underwater disposables for snorkeling)
"credit card" calculator (for exchange rates)
Sports Accessories (where applicable)
tennis racquet
golf clubs
hiking shoes
fins, mask, snorkel, regulator, and C-card
Non U.S, credit cards (Visa/Mastercard)/Traveler's cheques
   (no ATMs) NOTE: U.S. ATM AND CREDIT CARDS
   NOT VALID IN CUBA
valid passport (keep in hotel safe),
Cuban visa and necessary documentation (see Warning to
   U.S. Citizens)
driver's license

Cuba Superlatives

Best Large Luxury Resort (over 100 rooms)—**Hotel Meliá,**
   Varadero, Matanzas
Best Small Luxury Resort (under 100 rooms)—**Hotel Moka,**
   Las Terrazas, Pinar del Río
Best Romantic Hotel—**Santa Isabel,** La Habana Vieja
Best Boutique Hotel—**Presidente,** Vedado, Havana
Best Large Hotel—**Hotel Nacional,** Vedado, Havana
Best Small Hotel—**Los Friales,** La Habana Vieja
Best Room with a View—Top floors of the **Golden Tulip
   Parque Central**
Best Continental Restaurant—**Chez Merito,** Hotel Presidente,
   Havana
Best Cuban Restaurant—**El Aljibe,** Miramar, Havana
Best Seafood Restaurant—**La Zaragozana,** Havana
Best Italian Restaurant—**Restaurante La Floridiana,**
   Hotel Florida, La Habana Vieja

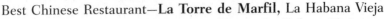

Best Chinese Restaurant—**La Torre de Marfil,** La Habana Vieja
Best Vietnamese Cuban Restaurant—**Hanoi,** La Habana Vieja
Best Lunch Spot—**Restaurant Gringo Viejo,** Vedado, Havana
Best Mojito—**Café Taberna,** La Habana Vieja
Best Daiquri—**El Floridita,** La Habana Vieja
Best Place for a Sunset Cocktail—**Hotel Nacional,** Vedado, Havana
Best Nightclub—**Ache Disco,** Hotel Meliá Cohiba, Vedado, Havana
Best Place for Nightlife—**Parque Central,** La Habana Vieja
Best Diving—**Maria La Gorda,** Pinar del Río
Best Snorkeling—**Maria La Gorda,** Pinar del Río
Best Golf Course—The only golf courses: **Havana Golf Club**
    (9 holes) and the **Club de Golf Las Américas** (18-hole),
    both in Varadero
Best Shopping—**Calle Obispo,** La Habana Vieja
Best T-Shirt—Che T-shirts at the gift shop at the **José Marti Airport,** Havana
Best Bargain—**Art** (prints and paintings; galleries
    throughout Cuba)
Best-Kept Secret—**Callejon de Hamel,** Habana Centro
Best Rum—**Havana Club Añejo**
Best Beer—**Hauey**

The Ten Best Beaches in Cuba

Varadero—Matanzas
    Powdery white sand, turquoise water, total tourist mecca.
Playa Girón—Matanzas
    Great scuba diving and snorkeling in a historical area (the Bay of
    Pigs, no yachts allowed!).
Playa Guardalavaca—Holguín
    White sand and coral reefs on the Atlantic—great for windsurf-
    ing, snorkeling, and diving. A tourist resort.
Playa Ancón—Sancti Spírtus
    White sands along the Caribbean Sea–side of a peninsula, great
    snorkeling and scuba diving, and not at all tourist-y.
Playa Sevilla—Santiago de Cuba
    Stretching the entire width of the province, white sands along
    the Caribbean Sea, includes Playa Sevilla, with its diving center.

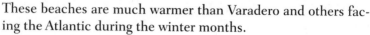

These beaches are much warmer than Varadero and others facing the Atlantic during the winter months.

Cayo Coco—Ciego de Avila

Miles of pure white sand surround this coral key, under the threat of destruction by overdevelopment of tourist resorts. Incredible snorkeling and diving.

Playa Santa Lucía—Camagüey

White sands for miles along the Atlantic, with dive centers to take you out to the reefs for snorkeling or scuba diving.

Maria La Gorda—Pinar del Río

Uncrowded white sand beach and sparkling clear waters, fantastic for swimming and snorkeling. Best diving in Cuba.

Santa Maria del Mar—Playas del Este, Havana

Best of the beaches closest to Havana. Relatively clean white sand, warm blue-green water with good waves. A family beach.

Playa Las Tumbas—Pinar del Río

Protected as a biosphere reserve by UNESCO, the very tip of the Península Guanahacabibes alternates between white sands and coral rock, where the Caribbean Sea meets the Gulf of Mexico. Not so much a swimming beach, as the water is rough, but hiking and bird- and nature-watching are at their best

Lodging and Restaurant Key

A Note about this Guide: We have used a number of symbols and terms to indicate prices and ambiance. Here are the code breakers.

Lodging Rates

☞ Rates are for high season—generally mid-December through mid-April—unless otherwise noted. Summer prices are as much as 50 percent cheaper.

☞ The following categories correspond to rack rates for the least expensive double room. Unless otherwise noted. Rates for singles are the same or slightly less.

☞ Tip at your discretion. Helpful taxi drivers, bell men, and housekeepers (leave cash on pillow) appreciate a few dollars. Unless you tip someone directly, the money lands in the manager's pocket.

Dirt Cheap	under $50
Cheap	$51–$100
Not So Cheap	$101–$150
Pricey	$151–$200
Very Pricey	$201–$300
Wicked Pricey	$301–$400
Ridiculous	$401–$500
Beyond Belief	$501–$600
Stratospheric	$601 and up!

Meal Codes

EP (European Plan)—No meals included.

CP (Continental Plan)—Continental breakfast (bread, cereal, juice, coffee) included.

BP (Breakfast Plan)—Full hot breakfast included.

MAP (Modified American Plan)—Full breakfast and dinner included.

FAP (Full American Plan)—Full breakfast, lunch, and dinner included (sometimes with an afternoon "tea" or snack as well).

All-Inclusive All meals, beer, wine, and well drinks (house brands) are included, most or all on-site activities, and usually tax and service charges.

Restaurant Prices

Prices represent per-person cost for the average meal from soup to nuts.

$	$0–$10
$$	$11–$20
$$$	$21–$30
$$$$	$31–$40
$$$$$	over $40

Touristo Scale Key

🐚 (1)

What century is this?

🐚 🐚 (2)

Tiny or no airport, or political upheaval keeps tourists away.

🐚 🐚 🐚 (3)

A nice, unspoiled yet civilized place.

🐚 🐚 🐚 🐚 (4)

Still unspoiled, but getting popular.

🐚 🐚 🐚 🐚 🐚 (5)

A popular place, but still not too developed.

🐚 🐚 🐚 🐚 🐚 🐚 (6)

Busy and booming; this was very quiet not long ago.

🐚 🐚 🐚 🐚 🐚 🐚 🐚 (7)

Well-developed tourism and lots of tourists;
fast-food outlets conspicuous.

🐚 🐚 🐚 🐚 🐚 🐚 🐚 🐚 (8)

Highly developed and tons of tourists.

🐚 🐚 🐚 🐚 🐚 🐚 🐚 🐚 🐚 (9)

Mega-tourists, and tour groups;
fast-food outlets outnumber restaurants.

🐚 🐚 🐚 🐚 🐚 🐚 🐚 🐚 🐚 🐚 (10)

Swarms of tourists and total development. Run for cover!

Rum & Reggae Mojito

The *mojito* is Cuba's national drink—the Cuba Libre (rum & coke) is a close second.

Ingredients
2 oz. good white rum
2 teaspoons sugar
Juice of 1/2 lime
Fresh mint leaves
Club soda
Ice (half a glass)

Directions
Mix sugar and lime juice in a glass. Crush a few fresh mint leaves into the sugar-lime juice mixture. Pour in the rum and ice cubes. Stir. Fill to top with soda water. Garnish with a sprig of mint. Enjoy!!

Rum & Reggae Punch

Are you dreaming of the tropics but it's snowing outside? Don't worry, you can create your own heat with this recipe.

Ingredients
1 lime
4 oz. water
2–3 oz. good dark rum (the stronger, the better)
2 oz. sugar syrup*
bitters
ice
freshly grated nutmeg

Directions
Squeeze the lime and add the juice and water to the rum and sugar syrup in a tall glass. Shake bitters into the glass four times. Add the rocks, then sprinkle with freshly grated nutmeg (it must be fresh!). Yum! Serves one.

---

*To make sugar syrup, combine 1 lb. sugar and 2 cups of water in a saucepan. Boil for about 2 minutes for sugar to dissolve. Let cool. Keep handy for quick and easy rum punches.

CUBA

Touristo Scale: 🗿 🗿 🗿 🗿 (4)

Overview

AN AMERICAN FRIEND OF OURS was on a "cultural exchange" tour of Cuba (which almost always means Havana and some outlying beaches). Actually, it was a *gay* group on an architectural tour (no, they weren't all decorators). So here is this group of 16 well-dressed, well-groomed, buff guys walking around Havana. As a perfect illustration of just how isolated life is here, all the Cubans thought it was a touring group of body builders.

On the other shore, we also have a distorted sense of what life is like in Cuba. When we think of Cuba, Ricky Ricardo and Fidel Castro come to mind. One led a band and kept a dizzy redhead nutty while the other led a revolution, still leads a country, and has kept a nation in ideological and economic isolation for more than four decades.

What are our images after Ricky and Fidel? The earlier ones are in black and white (like an old movie): Cigar-smoking mafiosi sweating profusely in their white linen suits as they overlook the card tables from the balcony of a Havana casino. Photos of JFK contemplating the Cuban missile crisis. A bearded Fidel Castro in fatigues and thick black-rimmed glasses shouting into a microphone, denouncing American imperialism as he jabs a forefinger into the air. Colors seep into the more recent images: Fleets of flashy powerboats overflowing with Mariel refugees and then desperate rafters crossing the Straits of Florida, all fleeing in hope of a better future. Then there is Fidel and, of all people, the pope in a warm embrace on the tarmac. Finally, Elián being taken by gunpoint to return to Cuba. So much history. Babaloo!

It seems like light years since Fidel Castro and Che Guevara rolled into Havana atop a tank in early 1959 to begin their revolu-

1

tion. The country's 30 year bout with Soviet-backed Marxist-Leninism ended in the early 1990s, leaving Cubans to ask themselves, "What now?" In the face of a collapsed economy, a huge part of the answer lies in tourism. Although most of those who come to savor the island's attractions these days arrive from Canada, Europe, and Latin America, there is little doubt that Cuba will again be a destination of choice for Americans visiting the Caribbean once relations between the two countries normalize. Americans will come as much for the country's beautiful beaches and the colonial and modern architecture as they will for its very special people.

Much has changed in the 13 years since our first visit to the island. As foreign journalists, we were constantly accompanied by a government "facilitator." The sight of a "gringo" walking down the street attracted many inquisitive looks then. Soviet-style food rationing was the norm. Empty shelves lined supermarket aisles. If they were filled, it was mostly with endless rows of one product, like Bulgarian plum jam. When speaking with visitors, Cubans were nervous and paranoid lest someone report their "inappropriate contact" with foreigners. The streets were empty, and fashion was at least 20 years behind the times. They had also never seen a dollar.

Visit Cuba today and you'll think you've landed in some poor capitalistic tropical country. Whereas the possession of dollars a few years back was considered a criminal offense, today everyone is out to make a buck. For better or worse, the liberating power of the dollar has been unleashed. Government–subsidized food is still rationed and somewhat scarce for Cubans, and there isn't much in the way of merchandise in the pharmacies or "peso" stores (as opposed to the "dollar" stores, for tourists). The good news is that the people remain friendly, sensuous, and seductive. The beaches are still as white and beautiful as ever, and Havana's colonial architecture, though quite decrepit, is still the richest in all of Latin America.

Change is in the air, and Cuba is no longer the place it was even a few years ago. Witness Havana's airport, with its new multimillion-dollar terminal, where gypsy cab rattletraps compete with spanking new taxis for your business. The cell phone company that caters to European, Canadian, and Latin American businessmen is open late and doing brisk business these days. Plush air-conditioned buses constantly pull up to the terminal's curb to ferry Canadian, German, Spanish, and French tourists to the most recently restored hotels in the districts of Old Havana, Vedado, and Miramar.

Although the number of tourists traveling to Cuba each year continues to rise (nearly 13,000 from the United States in January, 2001), the purposes of their visits have changed. For one, Cuba's socialism is no longer an attraction for left-wing sympathizers. Cuba's "great socialist adventure" has been put on hold while pressing economic changes take its society in a more capitalistic direction. Gone are the days when every Cuban had his job, food, vacation, medicine—even his wedding gift and honeymoon sojourn—ensured by the state. While the country's bankrupt economy has relied on joint ventures with other countries to expand its tourism industry, it has also forced individuals to find within themselves the strength and the wherewithal to survive in a world that increasingly resembles other developing countries.

Yet, against all odds, Cubans have survived the changes. Small-scale entrepreneurs have changed the face of the economy. From the *paladares* (small, informal restaurants operated by private citizens from their homes) to the *botero* (gypsy) taxis, Cubans are making money and learning the basics of Darwinian capitalism. In addition to paying exorbitantly high taxes, the *paladares* are strictly regulated by the state and officially are not allowed to serve shrimp or lobster, because these items are reserved for state-run restaurants only. Despite this disadvantage, the food and service at the *paladares* are almost always superior to the state-run establishments—and at a fraction of the price!

But the freedom granted to the people by the state has also taken its toll on society. For one, there are the *jineteras* (female hookers) and *jineteros* (male hustlers), the cornerstone of Cuba's "sexual tourism," the fastest-growing face of tourism on the island. *Jinetero(a)* literally means a rider, as on horseback. If you are male, *jinetera* will be one of the first words you'll hear upon landing in Havana. It refers to the young women—often they are students, salaried workers, or professionals, like teachers or lawyers—who entertain sexual relations with foreigners for money or goods. For women and gay tourists, *jineteros* are everywhere, too. In any other language they'd be "prostitutes." Like the Dominican Republic,

Cuba has increasingly become a destination of choice for "sexual tourists." The Cuban government cracked down on this at the end of 1998, forcing many to retreat from the Malecón (Havana's waterfront) to more discreet locations. Please note that besides selling themselves, the *jineteros* will sell you everything from a bottle of PPG—a "miraculous" sugarcane-based concoction that will supposedly reduce your cholesterol while working wonders on your libido (take that, Viagra!)—to their sister, to a box of cigars. (Beware! Many of these cigars are fakes. Even if you pay full price, it's best to buy them at the cigar stores and in the upscale hotels.)

With a population starved of American culture for the past three decades, Cuba will metamorphose overnight once the floodgates between the two countries have opened. Fast food, consumer consumption, billboards, neon, glass and steel will replace Havana's grand but presently forlorn state. (A friend who is responsible for much of the restoration in Old Havana told us that parking areas, for the tide of cars rolling off the ferries from Florida in the future, are now being included in the urban renewal plans for the Old City.) But for now, it's Cuba—catch it while you can.

Your point of entry into the country will most likely be Havana. A number of snapshots will become etched in your mind: the political billboards lining the roadways exhorting the people to stay the course; the dry staccato sound of dominoes smacking the Formica tables set up on the sidewalks in Old Havana; the "Detroit dinosaurs" rumbling by on a wing and a prayer getting lost in a cloud of mauve-bluish exhaust; the silhouette of the city's skyline at sunset as you drive down the Malécon; the waves battering the low-slung wall along the Malecón during the stormy months of fall and winter; the *jineteras* lining 5ta. Avenida or the Malecón after dark, waiting for a lift or a tourist who will take them out to dinner at La Cecilia or to dance at El Palacio de la Salsa; and the crumbling facades of the grand old buildings and villas in the districts of Vedado, Old Havana, and Miramar.

If you have the time, plan to travel inside the country, as there's a lot to see outside the capital. For one, you'll get a glimpse of what Cuba used to be like before the country shifted to a more market-oriented economic system in the early 1990s. You'll find that most Cubans, other than the city dwellers, have had very little contact with Americans. Believe it or not, you'll also find that many people still believe in socialism, Che Guevara, and Fidel.

Of course there is also the dancing and the music. Whether it's salsa, merengue, conga, cha-cha-cha, guaracha, guaguanco, boleros, rumba, mambo, sucu suco, or muerte-en-cuero, Cubans love to dance and to listen to music, most often at a ridiculously loud volume. There is seldom any need for an excuse to join a fiesta in progress or to start dancing in the street if your favorite tune is playing on some stranger's stereo. Once, several years ago, while traveling around the island, we stopped in a small town to ask for directions at the only house that showed any sign of life in the oppressive noon heat. A Willy Chirinos' salsa tune was blaring inside the house, where two young women and a guy were dancing and drinking beer. Within 30 seconds we were dancing and drinking beer with our newfound friends.

A Not-So-Brief History of a Complicated Past

In 1492, two weeks after landing in the New World (San Salvador in the Bahamas), Christopher Columbus "discovered" the coast of an island whose geography reminded him of Sicily. No doubt he thought he'd reached the elusive paradise of his quest. He christened the island Juana ("Jane," a name that fortunately did not stick). Although he described it as "the most beautiful land eyes have ever seen," he was searching for gold and there was none to be found here. So onward he went.

The indigenous Taíno population greeted the Spanish conquistadors with great hospitality and taught them to smoke rolled-up dried leaves that made them dizzy (tobacco). As in other nations conquered by the Spanish, the local population was evangelized at the same time it was stripped of its freedom and possessions. The Taíno rebelled. Among their leaders was Hatuey, who headed the island's first guerrilla movement. (A Cuban brew would bear his silhouette centuries later.) Hatuey was finally taken prisoner and burned at the stake after a three-month standoff. There were an estimated 100,000 natives living in Cuba in 1512. By the late 1570s they were almost all gone.

The conquistadors established the economy of Cuba with the introduction of sugarcane and slave trafficking (the first shipment took place in 1524); the island also functioned as a way station in the transport of gold from the Americas back to the Old World. It is estimated that some 200 million ducats' worth of gold, silver, and precious stones traveled through Cuba between 1540 and 1600. Sunk by pirates and hurricanes, some of these riches still lie at the bottom of sea off the Cuban coast.

Thanks to sugar, tobacco, and rum, Cuba's economy boomed well into the 18th century, much to the delight of the Spanish Crown and the Catholic Church, who together held a trade monopoly over the island. But the British, eager to expand their commerce in the West Indies, demanded that Cuba be allowed to trade freely with other powers. In 1762 the English navy lay siege to Havana, and after two months secured the capitulation of the city. After occupying Cuba for nine months, Britain agreed to exchange Florida for Cuba, and so the island was returned to Spain.

The United States has had its eye on the island since the days of Thomas Jefferson, who in 1809 wrote to President James Madison saying, "Cuba [is] the most interesting addition that can be made to our system of States." Cuba, with its thirst for slaves to work the sugarcane fields, was a necessary addition to the southern states' plan to spread slavery to new territories to counterbalance the abolitionist trend in the North. President James K. Polk, a southerner, unsuccessfully offered to buy Cuba from Spain in 1848. The South's interest in Cuba increased in the 1850s, when France and England ended their West Indian slave system, making the island the only one in the Caribbean still supporting slavery. And in 1857 and 1859, the abolitionist North had to step in to prevent Congress from seizing Cuba outright.

Although the importation of African slaves (nearly a million) ceased in 1865 (the African slave trade collapsed after the U.S. Civil War), slavery was not officially abolished in Cuba until 1886. Chinese and Mexican Indians were brought over to Cuba as indentured servants to fill the need for slave labor to work the sugarcane fields. An estimated 150,000 Cantonese found their way to Cuba between 1853 and 1871, when the import of indentured labor from China ended.

By 1870 much of the island's sugar production had fallen into the hands of American investors. Cuba became a crucial link in America's "triangular" trade. It provided sugar to the U.S., which sent rum to Africa, which in turn furnished Cuba with the slaves it needed to feed the booming sugar industry. By 1880, 83 percent of Cuba's exports went to the United States. Only six percent went to Spain.

It was the dawn of the "American Century," as Henry Robinson Luce called it, and Cuba's small economy became the testing ground for America's rising economic and foreign dominance in the 1890s. By opening its market to Cuban sugar early in the decade, it managed to make the island wholly dependent on U.S. demand. But in 1894, a Democratic Congress favoring Hawaiian sugar increased import tariffs on Cuba, making its sugar more expensive and thus less competitive on the U.S. market. Within a year the island's economy had caved in, unemployment soared, and rebellions erupted all across the island. By changing its tariff rates, the United States had flexed its new economic muscle and injured Cuba's pride, helping to unleash a nationalist wave that stoked the embers of the Cuban revolution.

Enter José Martí, the father of Cuban independence. Imprisoned and then exiled for his seditious activity, he moved to the U.S. where he founded a newspaper and the Cuban Revolutionary Party (Partido Revolucionario Cubano, or PRC), an independence-minded movement. As the leader of the PRC, Martí launched the final war of independence with a proclamation from his New York headquarters on January 29, 1895. The apostle of Cuban independence, as he came to be known, joined the rebels fighting the Spaniards on April 2. He didn't last long. Martí died in battle, riding his white horse near Dos Rios, on May 19, 1895. But his martyrdom was assured forever.

The big bang of both Martí's and Fidel Castro's revolutions occurred in the still waters of Havana's harbor on the night of February 15, 1898. Most of the sailors on the U.S. Battleship *Maine*, lying peaceably at anchor in the deep harbor, had already turned in when a powerful explosion ripped through the ship's ammunition hold, killing 266 of its 354-man crew. The sinking of the *Maine* was the pretext the United States had long been awaiting. Accounts written in Cuba, however, state the explosion was "considered to be a self-inflicted aggression to facilitate U.S. involvement in the Spanish-Cuban war." Cuba was being torn apart by the *independentista's* revolution against Spanish colonial rule. But after three murderous years, the war was now at a stalemate. War fever broke out across the U.S. within days of the *Maine*'s sinking. Images of emaciated women and children forcibly relocated in camps and in the cities by the Spaniards appeared daily in the press and underscored the urgency of ending the carnage. Congress and the public urged the President to join the war and kick the Spanish out of Cuba once and for all. "The President has no more backbone than a chocolate éclair," taunted a young and hawkish Teddy Roosevelt.

The so-called yellow press had a stake in the warmongering effort. "Remember the Maine!" read the newspaper banners. The day after the *Maine* disaster, a drawing on the front page of Hearst's newspaper, the *World*, showed the battleship at anchor in Havana's harbor atop an underwater mine connected by wires to a detonator in Morro Castle, the Spanish fortress at the harbor's mouth. Although an official investigations failed to conclusively blame Spain for the sinking, the United States nonetheless declared war by launching a blockade of the island in April. American military intervention in the war began with a brash Teddy Roosevelt, then Assistant Secretary for the Navy, leading the attack on San Juan Hill in Santiago de Cuba with his Rough Riders. Spain was quickly defeated after weak and haphazard resistance on the part of the exhausted colonial troops.

With American participation in Cuba's struggle for independence, the brutal and slow war between the rebels and Spain finally drew to an end in August 1898. Of a population of 1.5 million, some 300,000 Cubans would be dead by the end of the war. With this defeat, the Spanish crown effectively lost its last toehold in the New World, along with the Philippines, Guam, and Puerto Rico.

The economic boom of the 1920s fueled yet another wave of Chinese immigration, this time leading to the influx of some 30,000 Chinese men. Wilfredo Lam, perhaps Cuba's most famous living painter, is the perfect example of the racial integration that has been the hallmark of Cuban society: he is part Chinese, Spanish, and African. What's left of the once thriving Chinatown can be found in the two–block area of Centro Habana bounded by Zanja and Avenida Reina, behind the Capitol.

Cuba endured the tutelage of the United States for most of the first half of the 20th century, a domination that affected Cubans socially, politically, and economically. As a result, up until the 1950s, the U.S. ambassador was often perceived as being more powerful than the President himself. It is against this backdrop that a young, charismatic, hot-tempered, and fiercely nationalistic Fidel Castro emerged.

Fidel was born in 1926, the son of a moderately well-off Spanish immigrant landowner in the Oriente province. He studied law at the university in Havana and distinguished himself as a passionate and well-spoken attorney, full of *brio*. Hoping to spark a revolution that would overthrow the corrupt rule of dictator Fulgencio Batista, Fidel launched an unsuccessful attack on the Moncada army barracks, which landed him in prison in July 1953. After defending himself brilliantly in a much-publicized trial, he was exiled to Mexico by Batista.

With a group of friends that included his brother Raúl and an Argentinean doctor named Ernesto "Che" Guevara, (nicknamed for his habit of interjecting the Argentinean slang "che" into every sentence, meaning "hey" in English), Castro trained a small invasion force that eventually sailed back to Cuba in a leaky tub called the *Granma* (now on display at the Museo de la Revolucion) in 1956. From the hardscrabble peaks of the Sierra Maestra, Fidel Castro perfected his guerrilla war tactics, which led, two years later, to the downfall of the Batista regime.

Batista fled Havana in the early morning hours of January 1, 1959. A few days later, Fidel Castro rode triumphantly into the capital to herald the beginning of a new era in his country's history. But very quickly his reforms—which included expropriations and the nationalization of foreign properties and ruthless routing of his adversaries (long prison terms and summary executions)—won him few friends at home and abroad. His increasingly Communist sympathies and policies eventually led to a mass exodus of rich and middle-class Cubans and dramatically increased tensions with the United States.

These culminated in the infamous and disastrous (for Cuban exiles and the U.S.) Bay of Pigs (Playa Giron) invasion in 1961 and the frightening missile crisis in the fall of 1962, when the world was on the brink of nuclear war. His alignment with the Soviet Union forever alienated Castro from conservative American politicians. A trade embargo was implemented in June 1961 and, with the addition of the more restrictive Helms-Burton Act of 1996, is still in place today. But even more intense than the embargo is the utter hatred of Castro by most Cuban exiles, who will be satisfied only when his head is served up on a platter. These exiles constitute a formidable power base in New Jersey and especially Miami and South Florida. Who could forget the furor over Elian Gonzalez, who was shamefully made a cause célébre and poster child for Cuban exiles? Of course any attempts to lift the embargo are stifled by both Republicans and Democrats fearful of alienating such an influential group in two important presidential states (remember, electoral votes elect presidents).

Cuba: Key Facts

LOCATION	23°N by 82°W (Havana)
	90 miles south of Key West
	69 miles east of Haiti
	88 miles north of Jamaica
	132 miles west of the Yucatan Peninsula in Mexico
SIZE	About 66,666 square miles
	777 miles long by 119 miles at its widest point
HIGHEST POINT	Pico Real del Turquino (6,573 feet)
POPULATION	11,200,000
LANGUAGE	Spanish
TIME	Atlantic Standard Time (1 hour ahead of EST, same as EDT)
AREA CODE	53 (the city code for Havana is 7)
ELECTRICITY	110 volts AC, 60 cycles (although not consistent in hotels); Blackouts and brownouts are frequent.
CURRENCY	U.S. dollars. The Cuban peso (about 20 pesos = U.S. $ 1) is only for

	use by Cubans, although change is given in Cuban coins, exchangeable with same face value American coins. *No American bank–issued credit cards or traveler's checks are accepted anywhere. Canadian and British cards are O.K.*
DRIVING	On the *right*. For experienced and alert drivers only (risky night driving).
DOCUMENTS	A tourist card can be purchased in consulates and at the counter of airlines flying to Cuba. (*Read warning for U.S. citizens!*)
DEPARTURE TAX	U.S. $20
BEER TO DRINK	Cristal or Hatuey
RUM TO DRINK	Havana Club Anejo (5-7 year old)
MUSIC TO HEAR	Salsa and boleros, of course

Getting There

There are two main ports of entry into Cuba: José Martí International Airport in Havana and Juan Alberto Gomez Airport in Varadero. Both are located about 15 kilometers outside the main urban areas. Flights are frequent to both destinations and arrive principally from Canada, Spain, France, Italy, Mexico, Jamaica, the Bahamas, and various other Latin American capitals. The airports are notable for the conspicuous absence of the familiar logos of American carriers. You will also immediately notice the abundance of military and police personnel. Many have cocker spaniels. Well-fed and groomed, playful and well-behaved (not at all like the mangy mutts that roam around Havana), they are trained to sniff out anything suspicious, and race around (often unleashed) inspecting luggage and trashcans.

There are regular charter flights from Miami, New York, and Los Angeles, with tickets sold to approved travelers by agencies licensed by the U.S. Treasury Department. Potential travelers are screened for visa qualification. The preferred route if you're traveling from the United States is via Mexico City, Cancún, Toronto, Montreal, the Bahamas (Nassau), or Jamaica. **Mexicana** and **Air**

Jamaica are reliable carriers. Because you cannot purchase a ticket to Cuba in America even through a third country's airline, you must pick up and pay for the last leg of the trip at the service counter at your stopover. It is there you must also purchase tourist cards ($20 each way, to be stamped instead of your passport). Consider buying an air–hotel package when you book your flight, as it is required to have a hotel reservation at customs upon entering the country (for at least a night or two), and this may substantially reduce your costs. To avoid suspicion from U.S. Customs, it is better to go through Customs in the third-party country on your way home. This means not checking your luggage straight through, and perhaps a night or two stopover.

Getting Around

Upon exiting Customs, the visitor will be greeted by the din of animated conversation, honking taxis, and excited families waiting to meet relatives they haven't seen in 25 years. But what really is shocking are the old cars that are often available as taxis. Rather than hop into a spanking new Nissan taxi with air conditioning that will turn Havana into Anchorage, many choose something like a shiny black and sweet-looking 1956 Roadmaster. For 15 dollars, the owner will take you to your hotel or for a tour of the town.

Since Cuba is a huge country (about the size of Florida) and public transportation—whether it be train or bus—is very unreliable and not always comfortable, being independent is definitely the way to go. So if you're going to do Cuba outside of Havana or Varadero, the best way is in a rental car. You'll get to see the country, you'll meet people, make friends. However, a few words of caution . . .

There is only one highway in Cuba. It's called the Ocho Vias and stretches from Pinar del Río to a bit past Sancti Spiritus, about midway through the country. Although it is not heavily used—mostly because there are so few cars in Cuba—it can be hazardous. This highway is not I-95. There are no barriers to keep cattle from straying onto the (unmarked) roadway. Trucks often don't pull over to the shoulder when they break down. Drivers often use their horn in place of signals or brakes. After Sancti Spiritus, if you're going down to Santiago de Cuba, you'll have to drive on the busy two-lane Carretera Central.

In the city, be extra careful with the many bicycle riders with whom you'll share the streets. Bicycle riders are often distracted, and they don't have front or rear lights at night.

Car Rentals

First, bear in mind there is no competition to provide car-rental services in Cuba because government agencies—**Havanautos**, **Cubacar, Transautos, Transtur** and **Gaviota**—hold the monopoly, so prices tend to be the same. For example, per day cost for 2-6 days, the rates for an "economy" car are $45, for "tourist" $55, and for "luxury" $80. Because American credit cards are not accepted, you'll have to leave a cash deposit ($200 to $500, depending on the type of car, length of rental, etc.). Distances between important cities can be great, so go for the unlimited mileage option on the contract. Before you leave the lot, make certain that you go over all the bumps and scratches on the car. Car rental agents can be found in every airport, many gas stations, and in almost every hotel in the country. Gas stations (**Servi CUPET** and **Oro Negro**) can be found on the major roads, so fill up, because finding roadside service could be next to impossible.

Private Cars (Boteros)

Every Cuban with a car is a potential *botero* (gypsy cab). A trip from, say, Old Havana to Miramar can set you back $6. An official (state) taxi costs about $10. These are metered, generally newer models, ranging from Mercedes to Ford Escorts, and the fares are consistent, no need to negotiate. The Panataxis with 55 5555 on the sides are easy to spot, metered, and fairly reliable (the drivers know the city well). *Boteros* are illegal (thus cheaper) and the driver— often a well-educated professional with a low-paying government job—can be fined if he's caught moonlighting. Always ask the fare before you enter the car, negotiate if you feel it is too high. There are also taxis *particulares*, (see the license plate) or private taxis. These are usually the owners of cars who pay the state a monthly fee that enables them to function as taxis. Again, ask the fare first.

If you're going to stick to Havana, you could negotiate with some-one who has a car and arrange for him to pick you up and drop you off at your convenience. Beware of long-distance trips in hired cars as these tend to break down often. By the way, there are no tow trucks in Cuba (at least we never saw one!), and certainly no AAA.

If you're really on a budget, you can almost always hire a Cuban with a car for a day, to take you to the beach or to tour around a site (about $25). You may also be able to negotiate a weekly rate, which can run you about $400 for two weeks, gas included.

The other way to travel around the island is by flying, especially if you're going all the way to Santiago from Havana. **Cubana** (45-3133) flies from Havana to the Isla de la Juventud, Cienfuegos, Villa Clara, Camaguey, Holguin, Santiago de Cuba, Guantanamo, Matanzas, Las Tunas, and Baracoa. There are no intra-provincial flights. Note that flight times and dates vary widely among different routes. **Aerocaribbean** (33-4543) also flies between Havana and other provincial capitals, though not as frequently as **Cubana**.

In Havana, if you're travelling short distances, the cheapest way to get around is to hail one of the pedicabs that are always stationed near the larger hotels or at busy intersections. The CocoTaxis (lit-tle scooter-powered, open-air two-passenger coupes, bright yellow and in the shape of a coconut) are fun, too.

Telephones

Cuba is divided into provinces, each with its own area code. Often within a province there is a town or a city with the same name, but the area codes cover all of the other towns within the province. The phone numbers have varying arrangements of numbers, sometimes a 1, 2, or 3 digit area code, sometimes a 5 or 6 digit main number. If this is all too confusing for you, take advantage of the front desk or concierge service, or the Travel Agency desk in your hotel to make the calls for you. The country code is 53, not necessary within the country.

Here is a list of the area codes by province:

Havana	7
Pinar del Río	82
Matanzas	52

Varadero	5
Playa Larga	59
Cienfuegos	432
Villa Clara	422
Sancti Spiritus	41
Trinidad	419
Topes de Collantes	42
Ciego de Avila	33
Camaguey	322
Las Tunas	31
Holguìn	24
Granma	23
Santiago de Cuba	226
Guantánamo	21
Isla de Juventud	61

Calling internationally is a bit less confusing. Most of the fancier hotels have direct dialing from the room, but with surcharges. For a bit cheaper alternative, there are ETASCA phone centers, conveniently located in popular locations, where in air conditioned comfort you can buy a phone card (in denominations of $10s) and chat to your heart's content 24 hours a day. These centers are clean, brightly lit, staffed, the phones look normal, and there are little partitions between the four or five phones. There are also phone booths on the streets, but we had no use for them (even if they were clean).

The People

Cubans have some unmistakable, if not always endearing, qualities: They are happy, loud, passionate, animated, and vigorous in their communication, and make direct eye contact. Dramatic to the core, they'll often shout, regardless of whether they are inches away or down the block. Cubans are generous and effusive and will swear to die for you after a few drinks. People often try to engage in conversation on the street, to tell you about family members in the U.S., to take you to a *paladar*, to sell you cigars made by their father, whatever. Not everyone is a hustler, and many will befriend you to practice their English. Take the opportunity to ask for guidance in finding local places of interest, because as they themselves say, it's the neighborhoods and the people that will show you the real Cuba.

Because they spend as much time outside as they do indoors, life always spills over into the street, turning sidewalks into extensions of the living room, and often late into the evening.

Focus on Cuba: Hemingway's Havana, Walking Havana, and, Afro-Cuban Culture

Hemingway's Havana

Ernest Hemingway was Cuba's most famous American. They'd shout "Papa!" as he strolled from his room in the Ambos Mundos hotel in Old Havana to the Bodeguita del Medio, just a few blocks away, for his first *mojito* of the day. A winning number on any given day, this refreshing cocktail was supposedly Hemingway's favorite drink. It's made with white rum, raw sugar, crushed mint leaves, lime juice, bitters, and club soda. Later, after he'd won the Nobel Prize (in gratitude for his award, he offered the medal to the shrine of La Virgen de la Caridad del Cobre, Cuba's patron saint), he lived in Finca Vigia, just outside Havana. He kept his fishing boat in Cojimar, a short drive from his farm, where Gregorio Fuentes, a local fisherman, looked after it. Sadly, Greorio Fuentes passed away on January 13, 2002 at the great age of 104. We had lunch with him a few years back and were astounded by his lucidity and the strength with which he pounded the table when he wanted to emphasize a point. Gregorio was Hemingway's inspiration for the character in *The Old Man and the Sea*.

The best place to start learning about Papa's Cuba is the Museo Ernest Hemingway at Finca Vigia, at the corner of Steinberts, in San Francisco de Paula (91-0809). It's open every day except Tuesday, from 9 A.M. to 4 P.M., Sunday from 9 A.M. to noon. The house has barely changed since Hemingway left Cuba shortly after the revolution. The fine colonial-style house is surrounded by century-old trees. It is here that he wrote *The Old Man and the Sea*. His books, desk, and trophies are all still here. Outside, his ship, *Pilar*, built in Brooklyn, lies forever docked near the pool. Notice the rows of little mounds with crosses. They are all burial mounds for Hemingway's cats. Anyone who's been to the Hemingway house in Key West immediately will understand his affinity for cats—there are a dizzying number all over the house and grounds.

Next, head to Cojimar and have lunch and a cold drink at Restaurante La Terraza on Avenida Central. We like Cojimar a lot, and there is no greater pleasure than to sit down for lunch in La Terraza's dining room overlooking the cove after a day at the beach. Here ceiling fans cool as a well-dressed wait staff in tan suits glide over tiled floors. Or just have a beer and watch the spectacular sunsets. It is in this sleepy fishermen's village that Hemingway kept his *Pilar* moored. A bust of the writer adorns a modest monument near the old Spanish fort. Sadly, we will not be running into Gregorio having lunch at La Terraza anymore. The government considered him a national monument. He replaced Spencer Tracy in a couple of scenes in the film of *The Old Man and the Sea* directed by Fred Zinnemann.

Finally, take a look at the Marina Hemingway, at 5ta Avenida and Calle 248 in Santa Fe, 15 minutes from downtown Havana. Although Hemingway never visited this rather modern marina with its multiple canals, it is here that the International Blue Marlin Fishing tournament is held every summer. If you happen to be here during the tournament, you're likely to come across a number of wealthy American yachtsmen who have flaunted the U.S. embargo and sailed to Cuba to participate in the fishing extravaganza. The competition was originally sponsored by "Papa" Hemingway, who was gracious enough to invite Fidel Castro to participate in 1960. Of course Castro, the luckiest man in Latin America, won the trophy.

Walking Havana

Havana is made for exploration on foot, and it's easy to do. Our initial hotel reservation included a city tour with Gaviota Tours. Before setting out on our own, this was a great way to find our bearings, and put an order to all the landmarks. First, the van tour passes the important Government Ministry Buildings and Monuments. These include the Plaza De La Revolución, with sculptures of Marti and Ché), the Capitol, the Museo De La Revolución (with

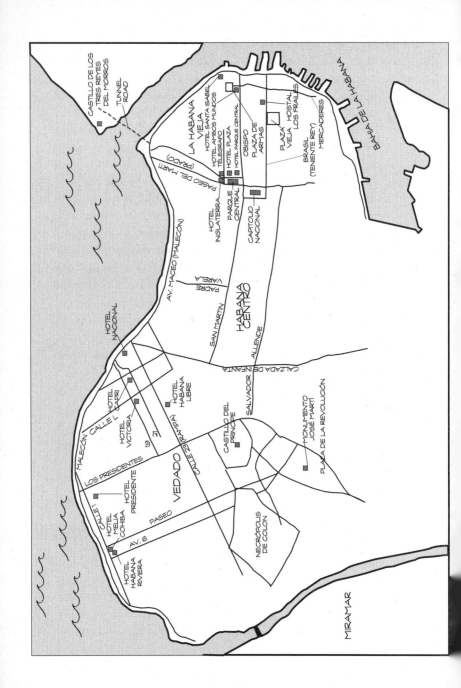

the tanks, planes and weaponry of Fidel's army, and the centerpiece —his boat Granma, replete with guards and an eternal flame) and the Malecón. In Habana Vieja, we disembarked and walked, linking together the plazas along the narrow streets. The Gaviota tour lasted more than four hours and included a running dialog full of history, trivia, and suggestions for all sorts of interests.

Walking through Havana Vieja you will find churches, museums, galleries, and workshops opening onto the streets, all welcoming tourists (with a rare admission charge of a dollar, but usually free). Cafes, bars, and restaurants abound, as do shaded benches in tiny parks. Many of the streets are closed to automobile traffic.

Cuba isn't really much of a shopping destination, as perhaps is Paris, but there are certainly things to see and buy. In Vedado, Calle 23 has shops and a small open air market. A film developing and supply store on the corner of O and 23 had the specialty batteries for our camera, at a better price than at home! The large hotels have shops and galleries. For diehard mall rats, the Plaza Carlos III on Avenida Salvador Allende between Retiro and Arbol Seco in Habana Centro (phone 33-8635) is an experience. Reminiscent of the Guggenheim Museum in New York, the building spirals up five levels, with a food court in the middle. Stores on every level include hardware, furniture, appliances, toys, clothes, electronics, and individual stores with items for $1, $2, and so on. The place is jammed on the weekends, and it is required to check bags before entering any of the stores.

In Havana Vieja, Obispo is the street with all the shops. You might not find anything to buy, but it is fun to look. Coffee shops and bakeries beckon. Some of the window displays could be described as *The Twilight Zone* meets Dada. At the end of Obispo (near the Floridita Restaurant) is a wonderful bookstore, La Moderna Poesia. Travel books and maps and picture books of Cuba are great if you plan to travel through the rest of the country. Reference books, fiction, children's books and political biographies and philosophies can all be found. Posters, postcards and lots of CDs (they will let you listen if you plan to buy) can all be had for extremely reasonable prices. For those who seek to impress the folks at home, cigars and rum can be bought at La Taberna del

Galeon, on Calle Baratillo, at the corner of the Plaza de Armas, next to the Hotel Santa Isabel. There is a rum-tasting bar, with bottles for sale ($6 and up). The back room is the place to buy cigars. Full boxes can cost you in the hundreds, but you can buy individual cigars, creating your own sampler. Cohibas are $6.40, Partagas $4, and Monte Cristos, $5. Next door at the Casa del Café you can buy coffee (a kg of beans is $17), related gift items (espresso makers, cups, kits), and rum singles. If you venture out to the plaza on a sunny day, you will find a secondhand book market with shelves of old books for sale; textbooks, political tomes, fiction, poetry, whatever. People also sell old stamps and money, anything with the face of the always photogenic Ché. Browsers and booksellers alike will engage you in conversation. Cross the plaza diagonally and check out the street cobbled with wood on the other side. The wife of one of the Capitan Generales who lived in the building there thought the sound of horseshoes on stone would keep her awake, hence the wood. Continue on Oficios to Tacon where you will find the outdoor crafts market. Ché berets, jewelry, sculpture, clothes, maracas and the like are yours for the bargaining. It is crowded and hot, so hold onto your wallet. Alongside, up on the sidewalk, are a great variety of paintings, prints, and drawings for sale at equally great prices. Anything from landscapes to religious inspiration, realism to folk art. Great variety, great prices. Be sure to ask for a receipt to avoid customs declarations hassles when buying art.

The Necropolis Cristobal Colón (also called the Cementario) in Vedado is a beautiful place to walk. With nearly a million inhabitants, this city of the dead is neatly laid out in a grid with alphabet streets and numbered avenues. Chapels, statuary, memorials and ornate marble headstones of the famous and the unknown as far as the eye can see. Admission is $1, from 9 A.M. to 5 P.M. daily, and a guidebook with photos, listings and a map (in English and Spanish) is available at the entrance for $5. See if you can find Papa Geraldo, the old guide. He gives the best tours.

Across the mouth of the bay, accessible via taxi through the underwater tunnel, lie the forts Castillo de Los Tres Reyes del Morro and the Forteleza de San Carlos de la Cabana. From up on the hill at the Morro Castle you get a panoramic view of the city, from the Nacional Hotel on the right to the piers in the harbor on the left. There are a few small museums up there, but it is hot and the guy selling sugarcane juice has only two cups and no running water. (Always carry your own water.) Farther down the road lies the Fortaleza, a much larger complex with a restaurant, gift shop, and nightclub. There is a cannon firing ceremony nightly at 9 P.M., complete with people dressed as soldiers in old-style military uniforms. This is a good late afternoon trip, to see both forts, tour the museums (the museum at the Fortaleza is bigger and has many historical artifacts, including some from the Revolution). Then you can find a good place to watch the ceremony before the crowds form (in nice weather).

Afro-Cuban Culture

Slave trade flourished in Cuba between the 16th and 19th centuries, as people were brought from West Africa to work the sugarcane. They brought with them their music, dance, and animistic religion. Naturally, the missionary slave owners tried to impose their Catholic system of beliefs upon the Africans. Not to be swayed from their own practices, the slaves used the images of the Catholic saints to represent their own deities and ancestral spirits (*orishas*). The largest Afro-Cuban religion is a combination of Catholic and Yoruba beliefs called Santeria. Yemaya, the goddess of the ocean and the mother of all *orishas* is identified with the color blue and represented by Nuestra Senora de la Regla, the patron saint of sailors. Chango, the Yoruba god of fire and war, is identified by the color red and is associated with Santa Barbara. Ochun, the wife of Chango and friend of Yemaya, is the goddess of love and rivers. Her color is yellow, and is associated with the patron saint of Cuba, the Virgin de la Caridad del Cobre. These are only part of the family of *orishas*, which are represented by Catholic statuary, draped in colored beads, featured in shrines and rituals (some involving sacrifice of small animals).

Cubans are very open about Santeria, and beaded necklaces and representative paintings are sold at the craft markets. Santeria priestesses, dressed all in white and smoking cigars, can be found in the big plazas and will tell your fortune (by reading coconuts) for a small fee. You will also have to pay to photograph them.

There are several places to get a closer look at, even participate in, the Santeria culture. In Centro Havana, artist and Santeria priest (*babalawo*) Salvador Gonzales Escalona has taken over the entire blocklong street Callejon de Hamel (between Aramburu and Hospital off San Lazaro). Found-art sculpture; decorated bathtubs sunken into the walls; Santeria shrines; a pit with small alligators and a turtle; poems, sayings, and philosophies painted in, on, and around walls, windows, furniture, street posts, every imaginable surface in every color; abstract, figurative, and imaginative styles are here. The artist's studio is at No. 1054 (phone 78-1661) where paintings are on display and for sale. On sunny Sundays the street is host to a big rumba *peña*, live bands and people dancing in the streets. It gets very crowded, and wilder as more rum is consumed. All are welcome, but hopefully it won't turn into a big tourist attraction. Visit during a weekday when you can enjoy the place in relative peace and photograph to your heart's content.

For the very curious, there is a ferry to Regla, a small town across the bay from Habana Vieja. Regla is the center for Afro-Cuban religions and home to several Santeria priests. The Iglesia de Nuestra Senora de Regla (directly in front of the ferry landing) is where you will find La Santisima Virgen de Regla on the main altar. This black Madonna represents Yemaya, the *orisha* of the ocean. The patron saint of the Havana Bay, the pilgrimage and procession with the statue (brought from Spain in 1664) take place on September 7.

The Museo Municipal de Regla has a branch next to the church, but the main section of the museum is housed at Marti No. 158, just up the street from the ferry dock. The histories of Regla and Afro-Cuban religions are told through exhibits and artifacts. Admission is $2, and the hours are 9:30 A.M. to 6 P.M., Monday through Saturday, and 9 A.M. to 1 P.M. on Sunday. The passenger ferry to Regla departs every 10 minutes from Muelle Luz, across from the intersection of San Pedro and Santa Clara in Habana Vieja (a small pier just beyond the three huge ones that dock the cruise ships and house the Customs Department, with the multicolored face of Che). The fare is 10 cents (or a 10–peso coin).

HAVANA
Where to Stay

"Cuba is Havana; the rest is just scenery," proud *Habaneros* (citizens of Havana) like to say. Our first impression is that the city urgently needs a coat of paint. Covered by decades of grime and exhaust, many crumbling facades are also in desperate need of repair. Everything seems abandoned, old, and distressed. Driving in from the airport, you'll see signs that distinguish Havana from any other Caribbean capital. For one, the billboards that read *"Patria o Muerte"* ("Homeland or Death") or *"En cada barrio, Revolucion"* ("In each neighborhood, Revolution") will be a clear indication you're not in your average tourist destination. The platoons of *habaneros* cycling everywhere (à la Miss Gulch) are a telltale sign of the country's energy woes. (Although things have gotten better in recent years, frequent outages and brownouts have wreaked havoc on home appliances.) The mass transport "camels" (semi trucks hauling cattle car–like trailers full of people) are a claustrophobic's nightmare.

While in Havana you'll be spending most of your time in the neighborhoods that run along the waterfront boulevard called the Malecón (sea wall). From east to west, the neighborhoods are Habana Vieja (Old Havana), at the entrance to the city's port, Centro Habana, Vedado, and Miramar. With its palacelike tenements, Habana Vieja and Centro Habana have been the city's poorest neighborhoods since the beginning of the century, Vedado has the faded glamour of the 1950's, while Miramar, with its opulent villas and gardens, remains one of the city's choicest. It is also the preferred neighborhood of foreigners and home to consulates and embassies. The city's streets are clean, with workers sweeping late into the night. Neighborhood revitalization is ongoing throughout (be careful walking under rickety wooden scaffolding and around piles of rubble), especially in Habana Vieja. Due to planning decisions that favored industrial growth in the provinces and rural areas early on in the revolution, Havana has been spared the sad fate of other capitals in developing countries—that is, the razing of its historical center in favor of modern glass and steel construction. As a result, Havana's skyline looks very much as it did in 1959—an added bonus for Havana's "retro" look, what with the old rumbling cars and all. Whether it be the Morro Castle, the top of the FOSCA building, the Habana Libre, or the Malecón, the one thing we like most about Havana is that the city still looks grand, regardless of your vantage point.

Attracted by the narrow and teeming streets, Europeans favor staying in the hotels located in or around La Habana Vieja. Among the preferred are the Inglaterra, the Plaza, and the nicely appointed Santa Isabel, across from the Plaza de Armas, smack in the heart of Old Havana. Our absolute favorite in La Habana Vieja is the Hostal los Frailes, located between the St. Francis of Assisi Cathedral (Basilica Menor de San Francisco de Asis) and the Plaza Vieja. Many of the streets in this area are closed to automobile traffic, making it a wonderful and safe place for a stroll, day and night.

Our hotel of choice in the Vedado district is the Nacional. Located on a hill overlooking a great part of the city, it is reminiscent of The Breakers in Florida. The Vedado distict, with its high rise hotels, grand old houses and its apartment building towers, is probably as central as it gets. The nightlife in the neighborhood is good and Calle 23, (La Rampa), lined with businesses and shops, is bustling during the day.

For a more sedate and out-of-the-way location, try one of the hotels in the tony Miramar district, though you may find you'll miss the proximity of the busy downtown. The upside is that the Miramar hotels have some of the best discos in town—not a negligible fact in a dance-oriented culture.

For those who are on a budget, Cubans are allowed to host foreigners in their homes (*casas particulares*). It is now possible to view and reserve accommodations online, as our friend Luiz (in Centro Habana) is creating a Web site complete with pictures and descriptions at www.viajescuba.com. Costs are usually very low compared to hotel rates, and amenities (air conditioning, private bath, etc.) vary.

One last but important note on lodging conditions in Cuba: Bear in mind that this country is only just emerging from the grips of a non–service-oriented socialist economy. The fact that a certain establishment may be rated as a five-star hotel does not necessarily mean it would meet such standards in places with an entrenched and competitive tourism culture. Unless run by an international chain (Spain's Tryp and Sol Meliá, France's ACCOR), the Cuban government runs all hotels. These are divided into groups, sorted by ratings, quality and price. At the top are Cubanacan, Gran Carib, and Habaguanex, followed on the next tier by the Horizontes Group, Islazul, and Gaviota. All of the hotels have "Travel Agency" desks where agents can book you into other hotels in their chain throughout Cuba, as well as arranging tours, transportation, tickets or reservations. Their markup is slight—only a couple of dollars.

Also, remember that American bank–issued credit cards are not accepted in any hotel . . . or anywhere in Cuba, for that matter.

Oh, by the way, Cubans are not allowed as "overnight guests" in hotel rooms in the city. Now, that's a real bummer! However, we have heard of stories where this rule has been flouted. Your Cuban guest will know how.

Old Havana—Habana Vieja

Hostal Los Frailes, Calle Teniente Rey between Oficios and Mercaderes, La Habana Vieja, Cuba. Local: 537-62-9383 or 62-9510, fax 537-62-9718.
e-mail gerencia@habaguanexhfrailes.co.cu

Only open for two months when we discovered it, Los Frailes is a jewel of an oasis in the often nonstop city. Only a few doors down from the Plaza de San Francisco de Asis, the theme is "Franciscan Monk." From the life-sized bronze hooded monk statues at the entrance and in the atrium to the background music of Gregorian-type chanting, from the frescos to the "monk" outfits and sandals worn by the staff, General Manager Ariel Fuachet has seen to every detail. Simply entering the beautiful lobby is a calming experience. With two floors of rooms and suites around the plant-, sculpture- and fountain- filled atrium, Los Frailes is small and intimate. The rooms are spacious and feature a well-lit sink and vanity separate from the bath, toilet, bidet room. There is TV with cable, direct-access telephone, a safe, a refrigerator with a minibar, and in-room heat and air-conditioning controls. Laundry services are available, but as with most places here, it takes 24 hours. There are candle-holders made of wrought-iron that match the electric light fixtures, as once again, every detail has been addressed. What really endeared us to Los Frailes is the staff. Friendly and energetic, helpful, thoughtful, and kind, they all really complement the experience—that and our free copy of the nationalist newspaper *Granma* (in English). Because it is so small, Los Frailes only has a lobby bar serving drinks and snacks. Breakfast is taken at a little restaurant at the corner, included with the plan.

Rates are *Cheap* for rooms and *Cheap* to *Not So Cheap* for suites. (CP)

Hotel Ambos Mundos, Calle Obispo, No. 153, at the corner of Mercaderes, Habana Vieja, Cuba. Local: 66-9530, fax 62-2547. e-mail: david@mundo.cu

Located a few blocks away from the Plaza de Armas and Parque Central in the Old City, this tastefully restored hotel is a good choice for its location, its history, and the excellent view from its rooftop garden. Tall enough to dominate the neighboring buildings, the rooftop terrace (Bar Parrillada Hemingway) is a fantastic vantage point from which to watch the harbor's shipping traffic and the hustle and bustle of the neighborhood residents in the afternoon. It's also a great place for that afternoon *mojito*. The lobby is large, airy, and comfortable with a beautiful bar for coffee or cocktails. A small establishment, Restaurante Plaza de Armas, seats 24 and serves créole as well as international dishes. There are 49 standard rooms and 3 minisuites, all with air conditioning, minibar, cable TV, direct dial telephones, irons, and safes. Their business center has phone, fax, and e-mail capabilities, but no direct Internet access. The hotel was Hemingway's home in the years before he won the Nobel Prize, and it was here, in a smallish bare room that's been preserved pretty much the way it was, that he penned *For Whom the Bell Tolls*.

Rates are *Not So Cheap* (CP).

Hotel Plaza, Ignacio Agramonte No. 267, Habana Vieja, Cuba. Local: 537-60-8583-89. e-mail: reserva@gcplaza.gca.cma.net

Diagonally across from the ever lively Parque Central, along with the neighboring Inglaterra and the Golden Tulip Parque Central, the Plaza, built in 1909 and restored in 1991, holds its own in stature and elegance. Between 11:00 A.M. and 1:00 P.M. the four circular stained-glass skylights cast beautiful designs on the lobby's patio. Enrico Caruso, Anna Pavlova, and Isadora Duncan stayed here in their day. The fifth-floor terrace offers a great view of Old Havana's rooftops and of the ornate facade of the Bacardi building across the street. There are 188 rooms, and while this is rated a four-star (remember, that's Cuban stars) hotel, the 10 year old renovation is showing its age. There is no pool. The front desk has fax and e-mail service, no internet access. Dance lessons are offered in the charming lobby bar.

Rates are **Not So Cheap** (CP).

Hotel Florida, Calle Obispo No. 252 at Calle Cuba, Habana Vieja, Cuba. Local: 537-62-4127 or 61-5621, fax 537-62-4117.
e-mail: reservas@florida.ohch.cu

Built in 1885, this beautifully and recently renovated hotel has an elegant lobby, with comfortable sofas and ornate chandeliers. Just beyond is an open air arch-roofed atrium; clean, quiet, elegant, and full of plants. The marble floor around it leads to a gallery, piano bar, and the Restaurante La Floridiana which serves Italian food. The Bar Café Maragato features live Cuban music. The beautiful and well-appointed rooms open onto the atrium, three stories high.

Rates are **Pricey** (EP).

Hotel Santa Isabel, Calle Baratillo No.9 between Obispo and Narciso Lopez, Plaza de Armas, Habana Vieja, Cuba. Local: 537-60-8201, fax 537-60-8391.
e-mail: comercial@habaguanex hsisabel.co.cu

After years of endless renovations, this cool, if a bit forgotten, hotel is one of the most tastefully decorated in all of Havana. The lobby is understated elegance, with plush couches, beautiful dark wood furniture, and blue beamed ceiling with large wood window shutters painted to match. The marble floored open atrium has a fountain and beautiful plantings in the center. Metal cage elevators carry patrons to three floors of rooms which open onto the atrium. This is where NBC chose to broadcast from during its coverage of John Paul II's recent visit. Use of their parking lot is included.

Rates are **Pricey** (CP).

Hotel Inglaterra, Prado, No. 416, at the corner of San Rafael, La Habana, Cuba. Local: 537-33-8593, fax 537-33-8254.

Despite its dark and dank interior and its not-quite-up-to-snuff service, we still have a weak spot for the baroque Inglaterra and its Old World charm. It's located across from the Parque Central and next to the National Theatre. The Cabaret Nacional, ($5 cover, with live Cuban music and dance DJs) with its doorway on the side of the theatre leading downstairs, spills music and club-goers close to the sidewalk tables where patrons may sometimes be accosted by neighborhood hustlers ready to sell cigars, women, whatever. Best rooms are numbers 115, 315, 111, 211, 107, and 207 (the last four have large bathrooms).The Restaurante Colonial serves breakfast, lunch and dinner, and the Sevillana Snack Bar is open 24 hours. The Terraza Bar on the rooftop of this hotel is also a unique experience. It is here that reporters working for William Randolph Hearst and Joseph Pulitzer would gather during the Spanish-American War to conjure up some of the best (and often fantastic) accounts of Spanish atrocities.

Rates are *Cheap* to *Not So Cheap* (EP).

Golden Tulip Parque Central, Neptuno between Prado and Zulueta, La Habana, Cuba. Local: 537-60-6627, fax 537-60-6630. Website www.gtparquecentral.com
e-mail: reservations@gtpc.cha.cyt.cu

This luxury hotel sits on the eastern side of Parque Central, between the Hotel Ingleterra and the Hotel Plaza. Built in detailed neocolonial style, 275 carpeted, tastefully decorated rooms and suites offer air conditioning, TV, minibar, safe, direct-dial telephone, and bathrooms with separate shower and bath. Dry cleaning and laundry services are available. The rooftop Greek-style swimming pool has a sweeping view of the ocean and La Habana Vieja, along with the Nuevo Mundo pool bar. There is also a dome-roof Jacuzzi, a sport and fitness center with instructors, and a massage salon for the body. The plant-filled multilevel lobby, with its double-sided central staircase leading to the mezzanine, has a very international feel, with conversations overheard in several languages. Several gay couples were spotted in the El Portico lobby bar. The hotel also boasts the moderately priced Restaurante El

Paseo, the gourmet Restaurante Mediterraneo, and the Alameda lounge where live Cuban music can be heard nightly.

Rates are *Pricey* (EP).

Hotel Telégrafo, Prado No. 408 at the corner of Neptuno, La Habana, Cuba. Local: 537- 61-1010, fax 537-61-4741.

Just reopened at press-time, the Telégrafo shares frontage on the Parque Central Jose Marti with The Ingleterra, The Plaza and The Golden Tulip. The eclectic façade of the lower two floors (the second was added in 1888) has been preserved and topped with two more contemporary stories. The upper three floors have a view of the Prado Promenade and the Parque Central, and house the guest rooms. The 63 spacious and high-ceilinged rooms are comprised of 6 suites, 6 junior suites, and 54 doubles, all beautifully and discreetly decorated with modern furnishings. As this is a Habaguanex property, all of the rooms are tastefully and comfortably appointed with high-quality amenities.

The ground floor lobby is stunning, with large interior stained glass windows, a huge ceramic mural–collage, water fountains, and a sunroof. A brick and stone arcade houses boutiques, a coffee shop, a snack bar, and a gourmet restaurant serving international cuisine round out the offerings.

Rates are *Pricey* (EP).

Vedado

Hotel Nacional, Calle O at the corner of 21st Street, Havana, Cuba. Local: 537-33-3564 or 65 or 67, reservations 537)-55-0294, fax 537-33-5054.
Web site: www.hotelnacionaldecuba.com
e-mail: reservas@gcnacio.gca.cma.net

Everyone knows "el Nacional." It's like saying "the Plaza" in New York. We have stayed in the Nacional for months on end and never tired of it. A late afternoon drink on the hotel's veranda has got to be the highlight of any trip to Cuba. Seen from the hotel's gardens, the view of the Malecón, the facades of the buildings along the waterfront, and the Morro Castle makes one feel privileged and serene. First opened in 1930 and restored in 1992, this Spanish-style hotel has hosted innumerable celebrities, including Sir Winston

Churchill, Edward VII, Johnny Weissmuller, Buster Keaton, Frank Sinatra, Ava Gardner, Marlon Brando, and others. In this very large building (eight floors), the 457 rooms, 15 suites, and the presidential suite offer air-conditioning, safe, radio, TV with cable, minibar, direct-access telephone, and hair dryer. For business travelers, the hotel offers an entire floor with an Executive Floor Manager and his staff, an exclusive front desk, fax service around the clock, bilingual secretary, translation and interpretation service, cellular phone rental, personal computers, car rentals, audiovisual service, DHL Worldwide, and breakfast, lunch and dinner served from the snack bar. There are elegant halls for dinners, parties, and cocktails. Apart from the executive floor is a business center on the second floor providing phone and fax services, with e-mail but no internet access. The little business center has its own bar. A gourmet restaurant Comedor de Aguiar, the buffet service Restaurante La Veranda, and a breakfast spot, the Desayunador, along with six bars and a Hall of Fame with traditional Cuban music in the evenings, make this hotel self-contained enough to offer a bit of sometimes necessary respite from the city. Two pools, the larger featuring a bar and grill with occasional live entertainment, landscaped grounds with tennis courts, and the Salon Parisien (a huge production in several parts featuring costumes, lights, music and dance representing the past and present influences of Spain, Latin America, and Cuba) round out the amenities.

Rates are *Pricey* (EP).

Hotel Habana Libre Tryp, L between 23 and 25, Vedado, La Habana, Cuba. Local: 537-33 4011, 3704, or 3706, fax 537-33-3141. e-mail: gerencia@rllibre.tryp.cma.net

A former Hilton hotel, the last and tallest (25 floors) built before the revolution and inaugurated by Liz Taylor in 1958, the Habana Libre was taken by Castro in 1959 as the revolution's headquarters. A suite on one of the top floors housed their offices. Now run by the Spanish hotel chain Tryp, this "luxury" hotel has a very frozen-in-time feel. The lobby is dominated by an open dark-wood staircase to the mezzanine which spirals over an amoeba-shaped turquoise pool with vertical jets of water. Frosted glass lights hang by thin cords from the second-floor ceiling. It is easy to picture slick-haired men in big-shouldered suits escorting bob-coiffed women in slender sheath dresses and spike-heeled shoes through the doors. Following the '50s theme are the restaurants: Polinesio (Chinese cuisine), El Barracon (Cuban créole cuisine), and the rooftop Sierra Maestra, which shares the 25th floor with the Turquino Cabaret, a disco with live music and DJs. The restaurants share the distinction of providing mediocre food. (Fidel was almost poisoned by a would-be assassin in the cafeteria in 1959. Some things never change!) One of the best-known hotels, the Habana Libre, was completely turned over to the press for the Pope's visit. The 579 rooms feature balconies, cable TV, the occasional refrigerator (friends had to climb the chain of command to the general manager to get the promised refrigerator moved into their room). The rooms are large and well lit, with beautiful views. There is a pool on the second floor, renovated in 2000. The business center (open 9:30 A.M. to 5:30 P.M.) on the mezzanine has internet access with four computers in private little rooms which rent for $3 for 15 minutes, $5 for a half hour, and $10 for an hour. The arcade of shops surrounding the entrance are convenient but overpriced. One would do better to explore the busy streets of Vedado for more variety and better bargains.

Rates are *Pricey* (EP).

Hotel Capri, Calle 21, between N and O, Havana, Cuba. Local: 537-32-0511, 3571 or 3747, fax 537-33-3750.

Run by the Horizontes group, this hotel is currently undergoing renovations through 2002. The hotel will remain partially open, but unless you enjoy construction obstacles, dust and noise, wait. The lobby is so fantastically tacky (all white and gold) one can only hope the redo will preserve this '50s rumpus room shrine. The Capri has 215 rooms and suites, currently decorated with what appears to be the original furnishings, and as the brochure says, "Its beauty is further enhanced by golden decorations and gorgeous lamps." The rooms feature the usual amenities; satellite TV, radio, safe, and air conditioning. The hotel also boasts a rooftop pool, lobby barber and hairdresser shops. Next to the pool, the Florentina restaurant has good, cheap Italian eats, and a view of

Havana to go along nicely with your meal. The adjoining Salon Rojo disco frequently hosts good bands and will remain open during construction.

Rates are *Cheap* (EP).

Hotel Presidente, Calle Calzada, No.110, at the corner of Avenida de los Presidentes, Vedado, La Habana, Cuba. Local: 537-55- 1801 or 1804, fax 537-33-3753.
e-mail (reservations): comerc@hpdte.gca.tur.cu

Built between 1925 and 1927 and being one of the first "skyscrapers" in the city, the Presidente has been lovingly restored by the Gran Carib Group to its original splendor. The lobby, all cream and black, with marble, silk, velvet, flowers, and brass, just breathes elegance. All the facilities have been updated in the 160 rooms, including two presidential suites, two junior suites, and two adapted for the physically handicapped. The rooms include fully equipped bathrooms, air conditioning, safe, direct-line telephone, satellite TV, minibar, and an audio system. Only two blocks from the Malecón, many of the rooms have an ocean view. The gourmet restaurant Chez Merito is expectedly expensive, you would feel out of place unless dressed for dinner. There is also a buffet restaurant, a grill-snack bar, a lobby bar-terrace overlooking the street, and a shaded Gran Café terrace out by the ground-level pool.

Rates are *Not So Cheap* to *Pricey* (CP).

Hotel Victoria, Calle 19, at the corner of M, Havana, Cuba. Local: 537-33-2625 or 3510, fax 537-33-3109.

This well-located hotel was built in 1928 (renovated in 1987) and retains its classy feel. While small (31 rooms), the rooms are well appointed and there is a small swimming pool. While restaurants and discos share the corner, the hotel is quiet.

Rates are *Not So Cheap* (EP).

Hotel Meliá Cohiba, Avenida Paseo, between 1a y 3era, Havana, Cuba. Local: 537-33-1254, fax 537-33-4555.
Web site: www.solmeliá.com

Managed by Sol Meliá, a Spanish hotel consortium, this modern, austere marble and glass tower with 462 rooms and suites is one of

Havana's newest (opened in 1994) and most expensive construc-tions. Located right off the Malecón and a stone's throw from the Foreign Ministry, the five-star Cohiba is preferred by businessmen (the 20th is the executive floor) and other fat cats. All rooms have air conditioning and most have ocean views. Rooms are standard, big hotel décor and come with satellite TV and pay TV, radio, mini-bar, hairdryer, direct dial telephone and Internet access, 24-hour room service and a pillow menu (a plus). No-smoking rooms and disability-friendly rooms are available. Restaurant Abanico (gourmet), El Cedrano (international cuisine) Habana Café, Labrasa Parrillada (grill), and La Piazza (Italian), provide a classy dining experience, and numerous bars offer respite. Other facilities include a swimming pool, a fitness center, a shopping arcade, and an art gallery. The Ache Disco is definitely worth a visit, even if you stay elsewhere.

Rates are *Pricey* to *Very Pricey* (EP).

Hotel Riviera, Avenida Paseo and Malécon, Havana, Cuba. Local: 537-33-3733 or 4051, fax 537-33-3738 or 3739.

If ever a movie of gangsters and other savory characters was to be shot again in Havana, it would have to be here, where arch-racke-teer Meyer Lansky had the run of the place back in the '50s. The décor is cool and totally in keeping with the tawdriness of the hotel's history. The cabaret used to be Lansky's casino, inaugurated by Ginger Rogers in 1957. The hotel's disco, El Palacio de la Salsa, always hosts the best salsa orchestras. The other Riviera venue, Cabaret Copa Room, is a bit smaller. While removed from the com-mercial areas of Vedado, you're right on the Malécon. The hotel was renovated in 1997 and boasts 17 stories and 330 rooms, fully appointed. Featuring international cuisine, L'Aiglon, Mirador Habana, and Salon Primavera restaurants, along with the 24-hour coffee shop near the pool round out the offerings.

Rates are *Pricey* to *Very Pricey* (EP).

Hotel Horizontes St. John's, Calle O between 23 and 25, Vedado, Havana, Cuba. Local: 537-33- 3740, fax 537-33-3561.
Hotel Horizontes Vedado, O#244 between 23 and 25, Vedado, Havana, Cuba. Local: 537-33- 4072 or 4073, fax 537-33 4186.

These two hotels, run by the three-star (that's Cuban stars, remember) group Horizontes, are pretty basic and similar. Foam mattresses, views of the alleys and airshafts, noisy air conditioning, TV with Cuban channels, hot water in the shower but not in the sink, and no water pressure to speak of (the toilets barely flush!), and the occasional loss of power are de rigeur here. The buffet breakfast is included. Our favorite looking dish was the spaghetti with bologna, and although we lacked the intestinal fortitude to try it, it was part of the charm. The fresh towels folded like swans added that lovely classy touch (not!). Both have small pools, bars and nightclubs. You get what you pay for, perfect for those on a budget who only need a place to sleep and shower.

Rates are **Dirt Cheap** to **Cheap** (EP)

Miramar

Hotel Copacabana, Avenida 1ra No. 4404, between 44 and 46, Miramar, Havana, Cuba. Local: 537-33-1037, 1263, or 1283, fax 537-33-0224.

Run by the Gran Carib group, this five-story hotel, with red clay roof tiles, balconies, and tan stucco walls is fairly standard looking from the outside. Directly on the water, most of the 164 rooms and suites (large and comfortable though nondescript) have an ocean view and feature air conditioning, safe, and satellite TV. The hotel also offers a business center, gym, tennis, a pool with sculptures and a bridge, a pool-side snack bar with thatched umbrellas, and a saltwater "natural" pool (no beach) created and protected by the sea wall. A woman rolling cigars in the lobby seems a little out of place with the bar and lounge areas and the noise they create. There are restaurants, a juice bar, pizza parlor, and a conference room. The Ipanema Disco completes the experience.

Rates are **Cheap** to **Not So Cheap** (EP).

Hotel Comodoro, Avenida 1ra, at 84, Miramar, Havana, Cuba. Local: 537-33-5551, fax 537-33-2028.

This used to be the old Yacht Club frequented by Cuba's social elite in pre-Castro days. It was a dormitory for Revolutionary Armed Forces (FAR) cadets in one of its multiple incarnations. This hotel's disadvantage is that it is rather far from the city's main attractions. However, the hotel's disco is still the den of iniquity that attracts the most beautiful *jineteras* in the city and the (foreign) men who "love" them. Decadence reigns here. The main four-story building, built before the revolution, houses 124 rooms and a two-story cabana houses another 10 rooms, all equipped with private baths, satellite TV, the usuals. The complex was expanded in 1990 and again in 1996 to include 328 two-story tile-roof bunga-lows, with kitchenette and refrigerator, sitting room with TV, and bedrooms upstairs in single, double, or triple bedroom configura-tions. Due to the great distance from the center of the city, the Comodoro provides a resortlike atmosphere with its small pro-tected sandy beach, shopping mall, tennis court, Karaoke club and Havana Club Disco.

Rates are **Not So Cheap** to **Pricey**(EP).

Where to Eat

Despite the hype that surrounds Cuban cuisine in New York, Miami, and other cosmopolitan cities, you won't be blown away by the food in Cuban restaurants and hotels. You might stand a chance of tasting some authentic Cuban home cooking in the low-key *paladares*, the small (12 seats max) restaurants that have sprung up in the homes of citizens trying to earn a little extra to make ends meet. The food here is often better than in most state-owned restaurants and costs a fraction as much, between $15 and $20. The cuisine in most state-owned restaurants is often consid-ered "international," while the *paladares* offer mostly *comida criolla*, typical local food including rice and black beans (called Morros y Cristianos, meaning blacks and whites) with chicken, pork, or fish (lobster and beef are reserved for the state-run restau-rants) and tostones (salty fried plantains). There are no sushi bars, Thai restaurants, Tex-Mex, or anything of the sort on the island. A few Italian expatriates have opened up restaurants here and there. And what's left of the once thriving Chinese community still serves up Chino (Cantonese)–Latino cuisine in their vastly reduced neighborhood behind the Capitol. Don't think you'll be able to go on a diet while in Cuba. Cuban cuisine is the product of a Spanish, African, and Chinese cultural combination. The food is well seasoned (garlic and onions) but not spicy, contrary to the cuisine of neighboring countries, and often fried (because much of the food is cooked on a griddle or cooktop, as everyone does not have ovens). Vegetarians complain that they have a difficult time finding dishes to suit their diet, especially as good fresh produce is hard to find.

The buffet-style meals in hotels are a good alternative to restaurant hunting, and if you choose to make this your big meal of the day, you can do pretty well for about $12 for lunch. For slightly over a buck you can take your chances with a burger and a soda in a Rapid, the Cuban equivalent of Mickey D's. *Remember, no American bank– issued credit cards are accepted!*

Havana Restaurants

Don Cangrejo, Avenida 1a, No. 1606, between Calle 16 and 18, Miramar, 24-4169. Built as a 1950s-style residence, this restaurant by the water is owned and managed by Cuba's Ministry of Fisheries. The seafood is therefore good and varied, if a bit pricey. For a fraction of the cost of eating in the formal dining area, you can have lunch outside on a sunny day (highly recommended) and watch the Caribbean lap up to your table. $$$.

El Aljibe, Avenida 7ma, between 24 and 26, Miramar, 24-1583 or 84. This is the place everyone goes to when in Havana. Their specialty, Pollo Aljibe, is basic: white rice, excellent black beans, french-fried potatoes and fried plantains, and a deliciously roasted chicken served with a secret-recipe citrus-based sauce called *mojo* (pronounced *mo*-ho). They do serve other dishes, but it seems that everyone goes for the signature meal. The restaurant, with its open-air thatched-roof design (complete with cats on the roof) is best for lazy summer lunches. Very popular with tourist groups, off-hours are best to avoid the noise and cigarette smoke. Find a hammock and a cool breeze after a meal here. $$$

El Floridita, Obispo 557, at the corner of Monserrate, Havana Vieja, 63-1063, 63-1111, 63-1060. In the same vein as La Bodeguita, this erstwhile Hemingway haunt hasn't changed its décor since "Papa" had his last drink here. Still cool, and still makes the best daiquiris (Hemingway's favorite here) in town. $$$

El Patio Colonial, Plaza de la Catedral, Havana Vieja, 33-8146. This old mansion with stained-glass windows and a beautiful fountain in the courtyard may be a bit precious, but the food is consistently good and the ambiance is always happening (and romantic). Lively music bands. Good for lunch and dinner. $$$

La Bodeguita del Medio, Calle Empedrado, No. 205, between Cuba and San Ignacio, Havana Vieja, 62-4498. Probably Havana's best known restaurant, immortalized by its "discoverer," Ernest Hemingway. The trademark scribbling on the wall and the claim to fame invention of the *mojito* bring the tourists in by droves. Food is hearty home-style Cuban, and overpriced. They charge for everything, including bread and butter. "A great place to get drunk," said Errol Flynn. $$$

La Cecilia, 5ta Avenida and Calle 110, Miramar, 33-1562. Another mainstay in the upper category of restaurants in Havana. This out-of-the-way but excellent surf-and-turf restaurant has a good salsa club. Dinner and a dance? $$$$

Le Select, Calle 28 between 5ta and 7ms Avenidas, Miramar, 24-7410. Located in an air conditioned mansion that was once home to Che Guevara, this restaurant is the top of the line and the most expensive. The service is impeccable, as is the food (old-style French). Dine indoors or at poolside in back. Come here to celebrate some extravaganza and forget about how much it costs. $$$$$

La Taberna, the corner Mercaderes and Tienente de los Reyes (Brasil), Habana Vieja 61-1637. This classy high-ceilinged room on the ground floor of a 1772 building is filled with beautifully set tables, brass ceiling fans and a massive dark mahogany bar, and hosts live music (several bands take shifts) through most of the day and night. Some popular tunes, some boleros (ballads), and the audience sometimes sings along. A very pleasant place to ride out the heat of the day or a thundershower (common in the spring), serving Cuban cuisine (lunches and dinners) and *mojito* after *mojito*... $-$$ (check the bill, they charge for everything).

La Torre, Calle M, at the corner of 17, Edificio FOSCA, Vedado, 32-5650. This restaurant with adjoining bar is located in the tower of a bunker-like apartment complex and has the best view of Havana. Good food and an unusually large selection of wines. $$$

La Zaragozana, Monserrate No. 352, between Obispo and Obrapia, Havana Vieja, 67-1040. Just around the corner next to El Floridita, this restaurant features Spanish cuisine, with an emphasis on seafood. Elegant and expensive, with a very attentive wait staff. Flamenco music can be heard nightly. $$$

Tourist-Cultural Complex Dos Gardenias, Avenida 7ma, between 24 and 26, Miramar. Right next-door to El Aljibe, this large tile-roof and stucco building houses several restaurants, serving Chinese, Italian, and Cuban cuisines. A nightclub (live music, different bands, open 7 nights, $10 cover), a French bakery, and an ice cream parlor round out the offerings. A convenient stop while walking through Miramar, admiring the parks, the architecture, and the embassies.

Havana Paladares

Aires, Calle L, near Universidad (near the University), Vedado. Everyone knows the Aires—we had countless offers from people walking around Vedado (surely they get a little kickback?) to show us there. By then, however, we had already found it ourselves, and had enjoyed a wonderful dinner there. In an old Victorian- style house, customers wait in the entryway on old red velvet couches, listening to the parrot chatter away in Spanish. Dinners feature (when available, no surprise here) roast chicken or pork, grilled pork or fish, and stewed beef (ropa vieja—meaning "old clothes," for its appearance) and include salad and rice and beans. Appetizers (a la carte) include the very wonderful tostones (salty fried plantains) for $1. Aires is open noon to midnight, but gets very busy at lunch and dinner. Try to stop in earlier to make a reservation if you are pressed for time, otherwise expect a wait. Open noon to midnight. $-$$

Calle 12, Calle 12, between 5ta and 3era Avenidas, Miramar, no phone. This *paladar* is good for its food and for the elegant decor of the turn-of-the-century mansion: black-and-white checkered tile floor, stained-glass windows, marble staircase. Calle 12 is a favorite with the foreign press crowd. $$

La Esperanza, Calle 16, No. 105, between 1a and 3era Avenidas, Miramar, 22-4361. This is the best *paladar* in Havana and attracts a rather sophisticated and independent clientele. It's run by Hubert and Manolo, a gay couple who have managed to turn their exquisitely decorated 1940s house into a warm and inviting place appropriate for intimate dinners or larger parties. Hubert, a former maitre d' in a Havana hotel, will fix you a fierce drink while you relax in the living room listening to old boleros. The décor is exquisite. A gilt mirror and elegant fireplace in a mint green and ivory parlor complement colonial-style rocking chairs and an eclectic collection of furniture and objets d'art. Reservations suggested. Closed on Thursdays. Dinner for two is about $40 plus tip. $$

Restaurant Capitolio, 1159 Calle 13, between 16 and 18, Vedado. Phone 63-4947. Another professional-turned-restaurateur, this time a lawyer, has turned his 1925 Southern California–style home into a profitable business, serving close to 100 people a day. The food is simple, the portions generous, and the whole house clean. The menu changes every day, and contains some diverse selections such as shrimp, barbecued lamb and rabbit, but as often is in paladares, not all items are always available. Open noon to midnight. $-$$.

Restaurant Gringo Viejo, 454e Calle 21 between E and F, Vedado. Phone 32-6150. Gregory Peck, the Old Gringo himself, holds court in this tiny restaurant from his place on the wall, in the big movie poster. Behind an iron gate sits this funky place with great food. Little tables and a little bar, movie posters old and new, stained glass and plastic vines lend the place its charm. Open noon to 11 p.m. $-$$.

Restaurante La Guarida, Concordia, No. 418, entre Gervasio and Escobar, Centro Havana, 62-4940, 63-7351. Fresa y Chocolate was filmed on location here in this beautiful (and well-worn, housing apartments within its four floors) mansion once owned by a well-known doctor in the pre-revolution era—you'll even find the old apple green refrigerator. Serving traditional Cuban food—fish, chicken, pork, (and the ubiquitous black beans and rice), along with some surprises like red snapper seviche and gazpacho. Lots of atmosphere. Photos of famous clients (Jack Nicholson and the queen of Spain, though not together) and movie stills line the entryway. Excellent for a tête-à-tête dinner. Reservations suggested. Open 7 p.m. to midnight. $$-$$$.

Going Out in Havana

Most of the heavy-duty nightlife takes place in the discos of a handful of hotels, most places staying open until 4 A.M. Gone are the old days when couples would spend the evening in a cabaret or at the hotel casino. Gone also are the days of the high rollers in town to watch the wild sex acts on stage. (Gambling is prohibited under Cuban law.) Although "dancing and a bottle of rum" are every Cuban's raison d'être, you'll find that the discos are filled with a wide array of characters, chief among them single foreign men with their pockets full of Viagra. Keep in mind that Cubans have a very open and healthy attitude toward sex and that not every Cuban is there to pick up a john or find themselves a sugar daddy. If you're looking for gay and lesbian nightlife, check with Hubert and Manolo at La Esperanza (see above and plan to have dinner), as they know the best private clubs catering to the scene. Officially, gay and lesbian clubs are outlawed. Hang-outs for cruising have been at the Yara Cinema (Calle 23 at L) and on the Malécon near the Fiat dealership, but the hot spots are always changing. Even if you don't dance and you're not interested in the meat-market scene, everyone should visit a disco once, if only for the people-watching and the human comedy. Jackets are not required anywhere, but a well-dressed foreigner will be appreciated. Some of the most outrageous places are listed below:

Clubs

Havana Club, Hotel Comodoro, 3a Avenida, at the corner of 86, Miramar. 33-5551. Cuban women are not allowed in alone, so gorgeous women may stop men at the entrance and ask for an escort inside. Once inside, everything is literally up for grabs. The music is more on the techno and pop side. Havana Club remains the ultimate den of iniquity. Cover: $10.

Palacio de la Salsa, Hotel Riviera, Avenida Paseo and Malécon, Vedado. 33-3733. The hottest bands play here and the club is consequently almost always full. Things don't get rocking 'til late. A favorite hangout of Havana's *jineteros* and *jineteras*. Open from 10 P.M. to 4 A.M., with a cover charge of $10 to $20, depending on the band.

Ache Disco, Hotel Meliá Cohiba, Avenida Paseo and Malécon, Vedado. 33-3636. Just to watch the people—how do they move like that?—is worth the $10 admission. And we love the name.

Club La Red and **Discotheque Scherazada**, Calle M, between 17 and 19, Vedado. These two small clubs are located diagonally across Calle M from one another. Both have live music and DJ's, both cater to a mostly Cuban crowd, both have a $5 cover charge. La Red has a bit more staid atmosphere and an older clientele, but a great mix of salsa, merengue, and popular dance music. Scherazada is popular with a younger crowd, with disco lights, tightly packed dance floor, louder and more techno music. Scherazada has "matinees" with a $3 cover charge in the afternoon for the students from the University.

Music-Oriented Venues

Casa de la Musica, 18 and 3era, Miramar. The cover is $10 to $15, depending on the band playing—and there's always a band playing. The Casa de la Musica is frequented by Cuban musicians, artists, and family and friends of the musicians, who come to take in the salsa vibes.

La Zorra y El Cuervo, Calle 23, at the corner of O, Vedado. This smoky basement (with the colonial maple furniture recognizable to anyone who grew up in the '50s and '60s) is the coolest jazz bar in Havana. Open late. Cover charges vary (between $5 and $15), depending on the artists featured and the day of the week.

El Gato Tuerto, Calle O between 17 and 19, Vedado. 66-2224. Right down the street from the Nacional, this gated little stand-alone building houses a club popular with a more mature crowd. There is a dance floor, and the music featured ranges from jazz to salsa, live every night and filled in with a DJ between sets. The bar is well stocked and the bartenders are kept busy.

41

La Tropical, Salon Rosado. Calle 41, between 44 and 46, Marianao. This place may be considered sketchy in some books, but Havana's proletarian youth love its weeknight (9 P.M. to 2 A.M.) live salsa and merengue bands. You'll probably stand out here as a foreigner, so be prepared to get hit on.

Sala Macumba-Habana, Tourist Complex La Giraldilla, Calle 222, at the corner of 37, La Coronela, La Lisa. 33-0568 or 69. This huge multi-purpose hall hosts big blowouts, very popular with the locals. Saturday, Tuesday, Wednesday, and Friday nights feature a cabaret show. Monday night is the fashion and variety show. Thursday is Salsa Night, and hugely popular, featuring the "biggest groups of the moment." Recordings from Salsa Night can be heard constantly throughout Havana (we bought the CD, so it can be heard constantly from our place too.). Sunday night is "Macumba en Carnaval," with a show and surprises. Open every day from 9 P.M. to 5 A.M. A bit of a long taxi ride, but the complex includes restaurants and shopping, you could easily make an evening of it. Call first for the schedule and reservations, or ask at the tourist desk at any hotel. The tourist agencies often run tour buses out to clubs outside of Vedado and Miramar for the evening, and can be cheaper than a cab, but you are at their scheduling mercy.

Other Options

If you want to peer into the past, check out the review at the **Tropicana** (33-7507), where you'll witness some excellent dancing. Note the special number with the dancers wearing chandeliers for headgear! This is the most famous of the cabarets, and the most expensive. With one drink included, tickets (which must be reserved) will cost you up to $85, depending on seat location. The club (open air) opens at 8:30 P.M. and the show starts at 10 P.M. Performances are cancelled due to rain, and money is refunded relative to the percentage of the show performed. Other cabaret shows of note are presented at the Nacional, Capri, Riviera, and Havana Libre hotels. Any hotel tourist desk can arrange a reservation and transportation to any of these.

And if you're really in the mood for something, say, more adventurous and impromptu, you can always hang at the different but

well-known *peñas* around town. Listings for some of the more organized *peñas* are in the free tourist magazine Cartelera, found in
hotel lobbies, featuring music and dancing of all types, popular,
folk, salsa, rumba, and boleros, to name a few. These are held at
such venues as the Teatro Nacional at Paseo and 39th, near the
Plaza de la Revolution, Centro Habana; phone 33-5713, and at the
Palacio de la Artesenia on Calle Cuba no. 64 at the corner of Pena
Pobre and Cuarteles, Habana Vieja. Sometimes more informally
held in homes or restaurants, Cubans get together for *el descargue,*
a sort of poetry and music slam/jam. Someone inevitably has a guitar and you'll be welcome to join in by tapping on a bottle with a
spoon. You'll be more than welcome if you bring a bottle of rum
along with you!

Last but not least—and free—is the Malecón, otherwise known
in Havana as *el sofa*, which describes its function perfectly. Built in
1901 during the American administration, the 8 km long sea wall
runs from Miramar, along Avenida de Maceo skirting Vedado and
Centro Habana, to the mouth of the bay in Habana Vieja. The best
place to sit is down by the Nacional or off of Centro Habana, where
you can while away endless hours watching life go by. At night
you'll likely to find a fisherman, a group of teenagers with a bottle
and a guitar, a couple kissing under the starry dome, a grandmother
selling *cerveza y mani* (beer and peanuts). Anything can happen on
the Malécon.

Beaches Near Havana-Playas del Este

The closest beaches to Havana are those to be found in Playas del
Este, which the Cubans call the Costa Azul, about 20 miles (Santa
Maria del Mar, mid-way down the coastal district, is 30 minutes
from Habana Vicja, 40 from Vedado- about a $20 cab fare) east of
Havana. The roads are reasonable and the route is straight and well
marked, so renting a car would be a reasonable choice. *Habaneros*
will do anything to get out to any one of these seven beaches during the summer months. Of the seven, Bacuranao is the closest to
Havana and Tropico the farthest. Between these two you'll find the
beaches of Megano, Santa Maria del Mar, Boca Ciega, Guanabo,
and Jibacoa. You'll find bungalows, villas, hotels, apartments (all

for rent) and restaurants all along the Playas del Este. Santa Maria del Mar is the best of the beaches, and probably the most popular. As in parts of Havana, the buildings are pretty worn, but many are undergoing extensive renovation. The water is warm and a beautiful turquoise. The beaches are relatively clean but not groomed. Lots of organic stuff washed up-seaweed, coral, wood. Some trash, but not too bad. Not too crowded either, even during school vacation. Plenty of families, couples, joggers, fishermen (who ply their wares at the restaurants right there at the beach), an entrepreneurial soul giving massages and doing reflexology under a thatched roof to salsa music, and police in uniform, on foot or four-wheel sand buggies, patrolling for thieves and U.S.-bound émigrés. There are small markets along the main street Avenida de las Terrazas, for snacks, drinks, groceries, and assorted sundry little items, and ETASCA phone booths, a health clinic, sports facilities for tennis, basketball, and volleyball (well worn but functional- bring your own balls and racquets), bars, restaurants, and open-air cafes under thatched roofs. Be advised that there is fumigation at night for mosquitos, and huge conflagrations at the landfills.

Where to Stay

Aparthotel Atlantico Horizontes, Avenida Las Terrazas between Calles 11 and 12, Santa Maria del Mar, La Habana, Cuba. Local: 537- 2188

One block (one parking lot, really) from the beach, this place would be ideal for a group of friends to stay. Lots of families, mostly Cuban, hang out by the pool (complete with bar and snack shop). There is a decent restaurant within (the entire meal, fish or chicken with rice and beans is about $3, a can of beer is $1), tennis and volleyball courts next door, and basketball courts across the street. There are 180 apartments in one-, two-, and three bedroom arrangements in three four-story buildings. For $40, we got a top floor apartment, with three bedrooms (sleeps six), two bathrooms, a kitchen, dining room, living room with TV (no reception, but it looked nice there on the stand), and balconies on two sides overlooking the ocean and the countryside. The windows and balcony doors had only louvered wood—no glass, no screens. No air conditioning, but with all the louvers open there is a fantastic sea breeze. The kitchen had a little cube fridge and a sink. The bathrooms had toilets with great water pressure. (They flushed! A big thrill after some of the places we stayed in Havana.) We had to ask them to turn on the lights at dusk, and there was no hope of hot water in the shower. A little like camping out, but much better.

Rates are *Dirt Cheap* (EP)

Hotel Atlantico, Avenida Las Terrazas at Calle 11, Santa Maria del Mar. Local: 537-971085, fax 537-961532.

Across the street from the aforementioned Aparthotel Atlantico and right on the beach sits this Gran Carib four-story, 192 room gated pink cement block. Many Canadian and European tour companies book here for a relatively affordable all-inclusive vacation alternative to Varadero. We spoke to one Canadian guest who was very disappointed with the place, and informed us that it had just been downgraded from three stars to two. The place is falling into disrepair (notably the air conditioning and the bathrooms), looking shabby, and with less than stellar service. Facilities include a swimming pool, tennis court, disco, buffet restaurant (serving all the meals included in the plan), and a car rental and travel agency desk.

Rates are *Not so Cheap* (AP).

Hotel Tropicoco, Avenida Las Terrazas at Calle 7, Santa Maria del Mar. Local: 537-2531.

This place will be nice when they finish renovations in another year. It's a little scary looking right now, all overgrown, with peeling paint, crumbling walls, and nobody around. Once inside, however, it shows promise, as you can see progress. Open during repairs, this Horizontes-run hotel has 188 rooms, offering various options regarding meal plans.

Rates are *Dirt Cheap* to *Cheap* (depending on the meal plan).

WEST OF HAVANA

If you're traveling west, take the desolate but picturesque north coast road (Costa Norte). Just outside Havana, you'll drive past the port of Mariel, which lent its name to the famous early '80s boat lift.

Pinar del Río is the third largest province in Cuba. Mountains, valleys, rivers, caves, plains, and beaches make for a varied landscape. While the best tobacco in Cuba is grown here, sugarcane plantations, rice paddies, citrus groves, cattle ranches, and copper mining provide for the people (via the government).

Pine forests to the west, semi-deciduous forests to the east, and a swampy and marshy coastline are home to hundreds of species of birds, both endemic and migratory. Paradise for birdwatchers. **Las Terrazas**, in the Sierra del Rosario is a planned settlement originating as a reforestation project and has been designated as a UNESCO biosphere reserve. **Las Terrazas** is also home to a gated tourist resort, with a hotel built in 1994, art galleries and workshops, an abandoned coffee plantation from the 19th century with a restaurant, many hiking trails, and the **Ecotourism Center**, where you can plan your adventures in the province. The mountain resorts of the **Hotel Moka** at Candelaria and the **Villas Soroa** just to the south are among the finest in the area.

Next to the **Villas Soroa** is the **Orquidareo** (established in 1943), which houses 350 species of orchid easily grown in this area of rainforest (open daily 9 A.M. to 4 P.M., closed for an hour at noon, $2 admission). Across the street is a beautiful waterfall, where you can swim in the pool at the base of the falls. Up the hill from the hotel, above the falls is the bar **Castillo de la Nubes**, with an excellent view of both the valley and the coastal plains (open daily 8 A.M. to 5 P.M.).

Heading farther west, the hot springs at **San Diego de los Banos** is a great place to rest and rejuvinate. The **Balnearo San Diego** offers baths (communal and private), and beauty and massage services. The sulfurous waters are hot (85 degrees to 105 degrees F) and potent, and only 15 minutes of immersion per day is allowed.

In the city of Pinar del Río, the provincial capital, check out the **Museo de Ciencias Naturales**, at Marti No. 202, located in the old

(1914) Palacio Guasch, a formidably eclectic piece of architecture. The **Fabrica de Bebedas Casa Garay,** on Isabel Rubio No. 189 between Ceferino Fernandes and Frank Pais, famous for its Guayabita del Pinar brandy made from guavas, has a tasting room and sells bottles of the sweet or dry versions for about $5 (open Monday through Friday, 8:30 A.M. to 4:30 P.M.). A visit to the **Fabrica de Tobacos Francisco Donatien** at Maceo No. 157 Oeste demonstrates the area's most famous industry as workers continuously roll cigars, which you can buy in their shop (open Monday through Friday 7:30 A.M. to 4 P.M., Saturdays until 11:30 A.M.). Visit the cathedrals and art galleries along and around Marti, then relax on a ride through the city streets in a *coche,* the popular old-fashioned horse-drawn carriage.

Just north of the city of Pinar del Río is the village of Viñales, known for its valleys in the Sierra de los Organos. Limestone hills (*mogotes*) rise from the green plains, and the geological effect known as karst (the irregular erosion of limestone, usually by water, resulting in irregular landforms, sinkholes, and caverns) give this valley its unique landscape. The hiking is fantastic, and for the intrepid, there are caves to explore, miles long, some with underground rivers. One such cave, the Cueva del Indio (once home to Indians) in the northern area of the valley, offers hiking and boat tours through the cave (lit by electric lights). For about $3, you can hike into the cave, navigate by rowboat, and emerge by a small waterfall at the other end. The area is quite touristy, very well publicized in the brochures, bringing busloads from Havana (about a four-hour trip) for day trips. El Mural de la Prehistoria is a yawn, and one of the first stops for the buses. The Horizontes Group runs both La Ermita and Los Jazmines in the town of Viñales, so if you stay in the area, you can plan your time around the tour groups and enjoy the landscape in relative peace.

It is said that Che Guevara headed the revolutionary strike force from a secret underground bunker in one of the area's mountains. Most of the Soviet nuclear missiles, which led to the missile crisis in the early '60s, were deployed in the Pinar del Río region.

Where to Stay

Pinar del Río

Hotel Globo, Calle Martí at Isabel Rubio, Pinar del Río. Local: 82-4268.

This charming little three-story hotel (42 rooms with refrigerator and bath) was built in 1917. The lobby is adorned with Moorish tiles. Locals come to hang out at the bar and take in the spectacle on the terrace.

Rates are *Dirt Cheap* (EP).

Hotel Pinar del Río, Islazul, Martí Final, at Autopista, Pinar del Río. Local: 82-5070.

At the entrance to the highway, there is not much to say about this modernish sprawling hotel (four-stories, 136 rooms with TV, radio, bath, pool, and a nightclub) except that when it's late and all the hotels are booked and you don't want to drive to Havana, this is the only place to stay.

Rates are *Dirt Cheap* (EP).

Viñales

Hotel Los Jasmines Horizontes, Carretera at Viñales, Km 25, Viñales. Local: 93-6205, fax 93-6215.

Good place to set up a base camp if you're going to tour the region. There are 72 rooms with TV and baths in two three-story buildings on either side of the pool, plus 16 slightly cheaper rooms called cabanas in a low building facing the valley. Niño Vera, who used to own the hotel, now runs the gift shop and will regale you with gossip about famous visitors. Stay in one of the cabanas is you can. The view is spectacular, and the pool area is often overrun with sightseers.

Rates are *Cheap* (EP).

Hotel La Ermita, Carretera at La Ermita, Km. 1-1/2, Viñales. Local: 93-6071, fax 93-6215.

On a hilltop east of the village of Viñales, this modern hotel has 62 rooms with balconies and bath, in either a one-story building facing the pool or in the two-story buildings facing the valley. The best rooms at this simple lodging are 51, 52, 61, and 64. The hotel offers tennis courts and horseback riding (for about $5 an hr.) and is within walking distance of the village.

Rates are *Cheap* (EP).

Soroa/Las Terrazas/Candelária

Hotel &Villas Horizontes Soroa, Carretera de Soroa Km. 8. Candelaria. Local: 85-2122 or 85-2041.

In this resort of green hills and tall trees sit 24 cabanas (in four-unit, single-story buildings) with comfortable beds, baths, and refrigerators. There is a grubby pool with a loud bar, ask for a room on the other side. Staying at the Villa allows you guest privileges at the park across the street (free admission). Next to the Orquidero and down the hill from the Castillo de la Nubes, what more could you ask for in a mountain resort?

Rates are *Dirt Cheap/ Cheap*. (EP)

Hotel Moka, Gran Carib, Autopista Nacional Km. 51, Candelaria. Local: 7-8601 or 02, fax 7-8605.

This four-star hotel, brought to you by the same group managing the Nacional in Havana, is nestled in the woods. A two-story building houses 26 rooms, each with satellite TV, refrigerator and bath. There is a swimming pool, tennis court, rowboat and rod rental (black bass in the reservoir), mountain bike rental, and horseback riding available.

Rates are *Cheap*.(EP)

Maria la Gorda

This place is named for an enterprising *zaftig* Venezuelan woman, marooned by pirates at the end of the Península Guanahacabibes, who used her ample charms and buxom physical being towards the "hospitality" profession. The entire peninsula west of the town of La Bajada was declared a biosphere reserve in 1987 by UNESCO. The Coast Guard checks permits to enter the Parque Nacional Peninsula de Guanahacabibes, available for $10 at the Hotel Maria La Gorda. Beautiful but rough seas (the Caribbean Current becomes one with the Gulf of Mexico through the Estrecho de Yucatán), hide the ruins of a "lost city" found at a depth of 2,100 feet, perhaps built as long as

6,000 years ago. Swampy along the north coast and rocky along the south, this area is birdwatcher's paradise.

The Hotel Maria la Gorda is also home to the dive center. While snorkeling here is excellent, it's the scuba diving that makes this place so well known. Many divers consider this the best diving in the world, with great sites near shore. Rare black coral lives in this area. Because this is Cuba, certified divers will want to bring their own gear (including BC and regulator). Resort course dives (beginner's without certification) are available at your own risk with the dive-masters. The dives cost $35 for one, $55 for two dives, and $70 for a full day's outing. There are many packages available, including night dives, up to $400 for 20 dives. Because diving certification is not required or available, the liability is yours, at your own risk.

Hotel Maria la Gorda, 14 km southwest of the guardpost at La Bajada on the highway. Local: 5771 or 5772, fax 7-8131 or 7-8077.

More like a scuba camp, this diving resort is more functional than posh, but certainly comfortable enough, and the only game in town. The small (40 rooms) gated resort is isolated down at the end of a very long road. Rooms come with TV, bath, and, air conditioning. Refrigerators are available in some of the rooms. Buffet meals are optional.

Rates are **Dirt Cheap** to **Cheap** (FAP is $20 per person per day).

Where to Eat

Cueva del Indio, Carretera de Puerto Esperanza, KM 38, Viñales, phone 9-3202. Located at the entrance of the cave serves baked chicken and manioc cakes at long tables, family-style. There is also a bar-cabaret in the cave. **Casa del Marisco,** across the street from the Cueva del Indio, is serving (what else?) seafood specialties. For an evening of all-out gaudiness, go to the government-run **Cabaret Rumayor,** the city's largest restaurant-cabaret, and disco. Their specialty is *pollo ahumado* (smoked chicken). Two miles on the road to the valley, **Rumayor** is open daily (except Thursdays) noon to 10 P.M., at Carretera Viñales Km. 10, Viñales, phone 6-3007.

La Ermita and **Pinar del Río** are in their respective hotels, and **Vera** is in the Hotel Los Jazmines. Standard hotel fare.

EAST OF HAVANA

Heading east, you may want to consider a four- or five-day trip. Starting from Havana, you can stop for a day or two in Varadero, the primary tourist area in the Matanzas province, for a swim and some sun. Expect to be sequestered away in a resort with lots of European tourists—not really the real Cuba. Then move on to Santa Clara, where Che Guevara's remains were finally laid to rest in 1997; and check out Remedios, Sancti Spiritus, and especially Trinidad, three of the seven colonial towns founded by the Spanish *conquistadores*. With their human proportions, these three towns are beautiful examples of the way life used to flow in Cuba's interior provinces. Don't miss the activity around the main square at night, were the locals gather to chat, play dominoes, discuss baseball, or just stroll. On your way back, stop by Cienfuegos and Playa Giron, the infamous Bay of Pigs. The diving there is excellent.

Varadero
Where to Stay

About 90 miles from Havana along the Via Blanca highway—about the same distance that separates Cuba from the U.S.—you'll come to the port city of Matanzas and Varadero beach shortly thereafter.

If by chance your plane landed in Varadero, you'll wonder if the pilot didn't mistakenly land in Cancún or Jamaica. The new postmodern hotels lining the waterfront have meticulously well-tended lawns. The pavement is smooth. The people are service-oriented. The sound of the gentle surf is barely muffled by the hum of the air conditioning that cools the hotel rooms in the noon heat.

What is there to say about these 10 miles of powdery white sand and clear turquoise water that hasn't been said before? A photo of Varadero hangs on the wall of every European or Canadian travel agency "selling" Cuba. The thing about Varadero is that although you're in Cuba . . . you're not. Everything is geared toward the sea-and-surf tourists, which makes it very difficult to distinguish Varadero from any other Caribbean sun destination. We recommend a brief stay here, if any.

One cultural site worth seeing to offset all of the commercialism is the **DuPont Mansion** on the Avenida las Americas. Designed by Evelio Govantes and Partners Architects before the revolution, the house and surrounding gardens are still in pristine condition. Tours are available and are a nice respite from the endless beaches.

There are literally thousands of hotel rooms in Varadero, and chances are finicky travelers will be able to find a few that are suitable to their taste. In addition to the Web pages mentioned earlier in this chapter, check out these web pages for more info on hotels and other facts regarding Varadero: www.cuba.tc/varadero and www.cubanacan.cu.

All the larger high-end hotels that cater exclusively to foreigners offer pretty much the same services: air conditioning, bars, restaurants, gift shops, pools, and water sports. Most were built in this decade and the architectural style is somewhere between postmodern and neo-tropical Spanish.

Where to Stay

Hotel Meliá Varadero, Avenida Las Americas, Varadero. Local: 66-7013, fax 66-7012.

Web site: www.solmeliá.com.

Built in 1991 by the same Spanish corporation as the Meliá Cohiba in Havana in a joint venture with the government, this luxury 490 room star-shaped compound is where Havana's diplomatic corps likes to come for naughty weekends. The hotel has all the amenities you might possibly need, including five different bars, four restaurants, a disco, water sports, two swimming pools, a fitness center, and tennis courts. It is also conveniently located next to the golf course, for which packages are available through the hotel. All rooms have minibars, satellite TV, and balconies facing either sea or gardens. The hotel sits on a rocky ledge with the beach a five minute walk away.

Rates are *Pricey* to *Very Pricey* (EP).

Hotel Sol Club Palmeras, Autopista del Sur, Varadero. Local: 66-7009, fax 66-7008.
Web site: www.solmeliá.com.

This horseshoe-shaped luxury hotel was inaugurated by The Man himself in 1990 as part of another joint venture between the Cuban government group Cubanacan and the Spanish hotel group Sol Meliá. The 400-room hotel is built around a large swimming pool which in turn opens up to a vast expanse of powdery sand beach. There are two lit tennis courts and a 24-hour pharmacy on the premises. Much like its cousin down the road, all the rooms in the Sol Palmeras have baths, minifridges, satellite TV, and balconies. About 200 rooms are available in the more independently styled bungalows, perfect for extended groups or families, although the beach near the main building is better. The luxurious and labyrinthine lobby with restaurants, bars, practically a rain forest of plantings complete with caged birds is worth a look.

Rates are *Pricey* to *Very Pricey* (EP).

Hotel LTI-Tuxpán, Avenida Las Americas, Varadero. Local: 66-7560, fax 66-7561.
Web site: www.lti.de.

This five-story pyramid built in 1991 under German management is named after the port town in Mexico from which Fidel Castro and 81 of his revolutionary comrades took off aboard the *Granma*. The 233 rooms are all equipped with the amenities befitting this world-class resort: bath, satellite TV, balcony or terrace. A good-size swimming pool, hot tub, floodlit tennis courts and the Discoteca La Bamba make the Tuxpán a good choice.

Rates are *Pricey* (EP).

Hotel Internacional, Avenida Las Americas, Varadero. Local: 66-7038, fax 66-7246.

This is probably Varadero's best-known hotel. Built in 1950 as a sister property to the Fontainebleau in Miami Beach, the architecture of the four-story Internacional is a perfect example of an "international style" that made its distinctive mark in Cuba in the last decade before the revolution. This hotel is right on the beach, and although smaller (163 rooms) and not as luxurious as those mentioned above, is an excellent choice and a good value. The décor in the cabaret and the main restaurant will make you dream of the "good old days" back in the 1950s. All rooms are equipped with showers, balconies, and satellite TV. The hotel also has a swimming pool, tennis courts, and water sports.

Rates are *Not So Cheap* to *Pricey* (EP).

Mecure Coralia Cuatro Palmas, Avenida 1ra, between 60 and 61, Varadero. Local: 33-7040.

This hotel has 200 rooms, all with bath and satellite TV, in a Spanish-style complex scattered in two- and three-story building blocks arranged around the swimming pool. Make sure you're not booked in the hotel annex across the street, which is a block back from the beach. Under French (ACCOR) management since 1996.

Rates are *Not So Cheap* (EP).

Horizontes Herradura, Avenida de la Playa between 35 and 36, Varadero. Local: 61-3703.

A more downscale but decent property, the 78-room Herradura is yet another horseshoe-shaped hotel (what is it with these architects?) on the beach in town. Make sure you get a private bathroom. Popular with Cubans, few of whom can afford the hip properties mentioned above.

Rates are *Cheap* (EP).

Hotel Ledo, Avenida de la Playa, between 43 and 44, Varadero. Local: 6-3206.

Don't expect too much from the cheapest hotel in town.

Rates are *Dirt Cheap* (EP).

Where to Eat

Varadero has more than 100 restaurants, most of which offer the same international cuisine. *Paladares* are not allowed to operate in this tourist town. Reservations here are an unheard of concept (except for the Universal and Las Americas). Among the notable restaurants are:

Castel Nuovo, Avenida 1ra y Calle 11, 61-2428. Italian-style restaurant serving chicken, beef, and seafood, as well as your basic pastas and pizzas. Opposite Villa Barlovento. $$

Halong, Calle 11, Camino del Mar, Near Villa Barlovento, 61-3845.

Good Vietnamese menu, only open for dinner. $

Lai-Lai, Avenida 1ra y Calle 18, 63-297. "Chino-Latino" fare like you might find in New York or Miami. $

Las Americas, Avenida Las Americas, 63-415. This restaurant is worth seeing if only because it is located in the library of the old Dupont mansion. In its prime, the spread boasted its own golf course, gardens, and private dock. The wine cellar and the majestic organ in the upstairs dining room are few of the "charming" details that only the out-of-sight rich could afford. Too bad the international cuisine does not match the décor. $$$

Las Llamas, Avenida 3era y Calle 33, 61-3488. Grilled meats. Open for lunch and dinner. Near Villa Granma. $$.

Universal, Hotel Internacional, Avenida Las Americas, 63-011. Exceptionally, reservations are required in this old-style restaurant. Nice environment punctuated by crystal chandeliers and Lalique décor. The house speciality is the Chateaubriand. $$$.

Trinidad

Backed by the Sierra del Escambray and facing the sea, Trinidad was the third settlement founded by the Spanish Conquistadores, in 1514. Sugar money bankrolled beautiful houses and buildings in the late 18th century, but as the plantation era ended, Trinidad became a quiet little village again. The railroad didn't reach here until 1919, and the highway not until the 1950s.

This isolation has made Trinidad the best preserved colonial town in Cuba. It is so unique in its conservation that UNESCO designated Trinidad part of its World Heritage program in 1988. Protected by law, old buildings and neighborhoods are being lovingly restored. Here the chickens, horses, and children all seem to have emerged from a turn-of-the-century silver gelatin photo plate (never mind the roaring air-conditioned buses that pull up to disgorge hordes of German and French tourists).

Much of what there is to see is centered near the slanting Plaza Mayor, the city's neatly designed square. The church is that of the Santisima Trinidad, of course, and the most recognized landmark, the tower of the former Convent of San Francisco. Four museums containing bits and pieces of the city's past can be visited near the square: the Guamuhaya Archeological Museum, the Municipal Historical Museum, the Trinitarian Architecture Museum, and the Romanticism Museum.

All the museums are located within a block or two of the Plaza Mayor. The Museo de Arqueologia Guamuhaya (Bolivar, No. 457) is open Sunday to Friday, 9 A.M. to 5 P.M., admission $1. The Museo Historico Municipal (Bolivar No. 423, open Monday to Saturday, 9 A.M. to 6 P.M.); the Museo de Arquitectura Trinitaria (southeast side of Plaza Mayor), is open daily between 8 A.M. and 5 P.M., admission $1. The Museo Romantico (Echerri, No. 52) is open Tuesday to Sunday from 8 A.M. to 5 P.M., admission $2.

The special cultural events in Trinidad are the Fiestas Sanjuan-eras, a carnival June 20–24, and the Semana de la Cultura Trinitaria in the second half of November.

Where to Stay

Casa del Campesino, Finca Maria Dolores, Trinidad. Local: 419-3581.

Twelve miles down the road towards Cienfuegos is this tiny and unbelievably cheap (think back to those youth hostel days) place to stay (it's hard to call it a hotel). There are 18 rooms in duplex cabanas, in single, double, and triple configurations. When musical groups stop by the restaurant there are "fiestas campesinas" with Cuban folk music and dancing. The admission is $4 but free for diners. Casa del Campesino also offers horseback riding for a nominal fee.

Rates are **Dirt Cheap**.

Motel Las Cuevas, Finca Santa Ana, Trinidad. Local: 419-4013.

About two miles northeast of town, this uninteresting 112 room hotel is frequented by tourists in buses. There is a pool and all rooms have baths. The rooms are divided into several buildings. Avoid the one by the pool, the favorite of the noisy tourists. There is a cave on the premises, Cueva La Maravillosa, accessible by stairway. You can't miss it, there's a huge tree growing up out of the cave through a large pit nearby.

Rates are *Dirt Cheap* (EP).

Where to Eat

Restaurante El Marino. Cienfuegos and Frank Pais. This favorite with the locals turns into a disco Saturday nights from 9:30 p.m. to 2 A.M. and Sunday 9:30 P.M. to midnight. $.

Taberna La Canchachara, Ruben Martinez Villena at Ciro Redondo. Local musicians play to a crowd of tourists and locals in this 17th century building. Things can get quite lively when drinking the bar's signature cocktail, the canchachara, made with rum, honey, lemons and water. $.

You'll also find a host of local citizens around town who rent out rooms at very modest prices. Same goes for the *paladares.* Check out Carmen Luisa Font's *paladar* at Simón Bolívar, No. 506, between Juan Márquez and Fernando Echaverri.

Santigo De Cuba

Santiago de Cuba is the island's second largest city. It has a lot more in common with the rest of the Caribbean than with its rival, Havana. Sort of like a NYC vs. LA thing, this competition goes back a long way. Santiago was the island's first seat of power. The revolution began in Santiago and ended in Havana. Santiago's racial composition is principally black while Havana's is mostly white. Santiagueros speak in a singsong fashion, *habaneros* don't. Santiago has an unquestionable and unique tropical flavor.

There is plenty to see in Santiago de Cuba, including San Juan Hill (Teddy Roosevelt and his Rough Rider's triumph, although notice how the inscriptions have been removed from the bronze statue), the Bacardí Rum factory (Emelio Bacardí y Moreau was the first mayor of Santiago de Cuba), Pico Turquino (the highest point in Cuba), and the music. The Festival of Caribbean Culture is held in early June or July, the Bolero de Oro is in August. *Son*, the precursor of salsa, was invented here. The best places to catch folk music are at the Casa de la Trova (Heredia No. 208) and the Patio Los Dos Arboles (Francisco Perez Carbo No.5 on the east side of the Plaza de Marte) where groups play for tips. The Ballet Folklorico Cutumba (Saco No. 170, upstairs, between Corona and

Padre Pico, phone: 2-5860) is the place for Afro-Cuban folk dancing. Sunday mornings at 10:30 a.m. is a dance show not to be
missed, for a mere $3.

Most of the city's action, day and night, can be found around the
downtown Parque Cespedes. On one side of the square is the mansion of Diego Velazquez, the island's first governor, currently the
seat of the Colonial Art Museum. Overlooking Parque Cespedes,
the Hotel Casa Grande, on the other side of the square, was *the*
meeting point of the city's bourgeoisie in the olden days. Take a
stroll down Calle Heredia, off Parque Cespedes, where you'll get a
good feel for the people of Santiago as they go about their business.

Where to Stay

Hotel Casa Granda, Calle Heredia, No. 201, at the corner of San
Pedro, Santiago de Cuba. Local: 5-3021, fax 8-6035.

The dean of hotels in Santiago, the Casa Granda, run by Gran
Carib, is equivalent in stature to the Nacional or the Inglaterra in
Havana. The hotel and Parque Cespedes are ground zero for Santi-
ago's social life. The view from the rooftop deck is excellent.

Rates are *Not so Cheap* to *Pricey*(EP).

Meliá Santiago de Cuba, Avenida de las Americas between 4ta
and Avenida Manduley, Santiago de Cuba. Local: 8-7107, fax 8-
7270.
Web site: www.solmeliá.com.

Run by the Meliá chain (of the Cohiba in Havana) in partner-
ship with Cubanacán, this is a five-star luxury hotel.

Rates are *Not So Cheap* to *Pricey* (EP).

Horizontes Las Américas, Avenida de las Américas and General
Cebreco, Santiago de Cuba. Local: 4-2011, fax: 8-7075.

Built in 1991, this postmodern structure is painted in a scream-
ing red, white, and blue. Basic and comfortable, standard for a
Horizontes property.

Rates are *Cheap*.

Where to Eat

1900, San Basilio No. 354, 2-3507. This former Bacardi spread is the best-known restaurant in Santiago today. The restaurant is also the training ground for the gastronomical school. International and Cuban menu. Open Tuesday to Sunday 1 to 3 P.M., and 6 P.M. to midnight. $$.

Restaurante El Morro, Carretera al Morro, Km. 9, 9-1576. Located six miles out of town, next to the Morro fortress at the mouth of Santiago Bay, this is good for a no-frills lunch. $.

Don't Miss

Cayo Coco Key—Unfortunately, overdevelopment of these tourist resorts has resulted in both omnipresent construction and the destruction of natural waterways. The opening of an international airport will only hasten the demise of the delicate balance of the marine ecology.

Baracoa—Toward the eastern tip of the island in the Guantanamo province you can visit Baracoa, a delicious little seaside town that's forgotten by everyone and retains an imaginary, otherworldly feel. Stay in the fortress El Castillo de Seboruco (now the Hotel Le Castillo) on the top of the hill overlooking the town. You can't miss it.

Santa Clara—The city of Santa Clara may not appeal to everyone. It is close to neither beaches nor mountains, but this midsize provincial town seems perfectly happy and oblivious of the outside world. We love hanging out in Parque Vidal late in the afternoon, when old-timers and lovers gather and children in their homemade carts careen around the park's pathways. Buy an ice cream and take a seat on one of the concrete benches across from the Hotel Santa Clara Libre (Parque Vidal#6, between Trista and Padre Chao, phone: 27548) and just watch life go by. The rooftop terrace has a great view of the city. Santa Clara is hallowed ground for Che Guevara buffs. The town is the site of his most famous battle (check out the well-preserved pockmarks on the Santa Clara Libre's facade and the Museo and Monumento del Tren Blindado) and the resting place of his recently discovered and much revered bones. The Museo Memorial Ernesto Che Guevara in the Plaza de la Revolution Che Guevara on the Carretera Central ties it together with all you could ever want to know about this favorite revolutionary.

INDEX

INDEX

Write to Rum & Reggae

Dear *Rum & Reggae Caribbean* Readers,

We really do appreciate and value your comments, suggestions, or information about anything new or exciting in the Caribbean. We'd love to hear about your experiences, good and bad, while you were in the tropics. Your feedback helps us shape the next edition. So please let us hear from you. Here's how:

Visit our Web site at: www.rumreggae.com
e-mail us at yahmon@rumreggae.com
or write to:

Mr. Yah Mon
Rum & Reggae Guidebooks
P.O. Box 152
Prides Crossing, MA 01965

Sincerely,

Jonathan Runge

P.S.—We often mention cocktails, drinking, and other things in this book. We certainly do not mean to offend any nondrinkers or those in recovery. Please don't take offense—rum and its relatives are not a requirement for a successful vacation in the Caribbean.

The Author

JONATHAN RUNGE is the author of ten other travel books: *Rum & Reggae's Caribbean* (2002), *Rum & Reggae's Puerto Rico* (2002), *Rum & Reggae's Dominican Republic* (2002), *Rum & Reggae's Cuba* (2002), *Rum & Reggae's Hawai'i* (2001), *Rum & Reggae's Caribbean* 2000, *Rum & Reggae's Caribbean: The Insider's Guide to the Caribbean* (1993); *Hot on Hawai'i, The Definitive Guide to the Aloha State* (1989); *Rum & Reggae, What's Hot and What's Not in the Caribbean* (1988); and *Ski Party! The Skier's Guide to the Good Life*, co-authored with Steve Deschenes (1985). Jonathan has written for *Men's Journal, Outside, National Geographic Traveler, Out, Skiing, Boston,* and other magazines. Future books to be published in 2002 from Jonathan Runge include *Rum & Reggae's Brasil.*